KIT & CABOODLE

FOR KAREN
Nothing Else Matters

Pitch Publishing Ltd
9 Donnington Park
85 Birdham Road
Chichester
West Sussex
PO20 7AJ

Email: info@pitchpublishing.co.uk
Web: www.pitchpublishing.co.uk

First published by Pitch Publishing 2022
Text © 2022 Matthew Riley

1

A CIP catalogue record for this book is available from the British Library.

13-digit ISBN: 9781801501514
Design and typesetting by Olner Pro Sport Media. Visit www.olnerpsm.co.uk
Printed in India by Replika Press

Matt Riley

Foreword
Kevin Day

KIT
&
CABOODLE

Football's Shirt Stories

I am a Crystal Palace fan

Matt, the author of this brilliant book, is an Aston Villa fan.

That means we automatically have a spiritual link because, in 1905, a young man called Edmund Goodman left Villa to become the secretary and manager of the newly formed south London club. He took with him (hopefully with permission) a full set of (hopefully washed) Villa shirts and Palace played in claret and blue for the next 70 years.

As it happens, it now seems that CPFC may actually have been formed in 1861 and our original kit was actually sky blue and white halves. The club have just released that as a 'tribute third kit' and some fans are very unhappy. Why? Because it's not traditional. As far as they are concerned, our traditional kit is the red and blue stripes introduced in 1973 in a bizarre attempt to emulate Barcelona. So far, I'm sad to say, it hasn't worked.

As far as I'm concerned, however, our traditional kit is the claret and blue stripes I remember from my childhood, and the only reason I still do EuroMillions is in a vain attempt to win enough money to buy the club and undo the terrible wrong done to our kit all those years ago.

All of which is a roundabout way of saying that, to football fans, kits matter. Colours matter. Badges matter. Crests and mottoes matter. Nicknames matter.

I am always being accused of over-romanticising football's place in the community and its importance to fans; but for me, each club is a living slice of (mostly) working-class history. Its kit, badge and nickname reminders of a proud tradition that is (mostly) long gone.

Norwich City are not called the Canaries because their shirts are yellow. The shirts are yellow because Huguenot weavers who settled there liked canaries for company and the area became famous for breeding them.

Chelsea's royal blue and white were the racing colours of Lord Chelsea. In the late 19th century Wycombe Wanderers chose the mix of Oxford blue and Cambridge blue that they still wear today. No one knows quite why they chose those colours. It may have been deference, it may have been aspirational, it may have been that the local shop had a sale on; the important thing is they still wear them and there would be trouble if the club tried to change them.

Don't believe me? Around 1910, Cardiff City decided that an all-blue kit would look smarter than the orange and brown effort they had been wearing. Shortly afterwards, a play called *The Bluebirds* was a smash-hit in the city and the fans adopted that as their club's nickname. Probably. And that's how things were until 2010 when their new Malaysian owners decided that red was a luckier colour than blue and a scary dragon would be a better badge than a weedy little bird.

It was a move met with genuine fury by fans. Season tickets went unsold and there were angry demonstrations around the city and the ground for as long as it took for the owners to rectify their error.

As I said, kits matter. Cardiff will always be the Bluebirds. Wycombe will always be the Chairboys, for the simple reason that the town was famous for making chairs. Likewise Walsall and saddles, Luton and hats, Sheffield United and blades. The list goes on.

My club are now, famously, the Eagles, because when we nicked Barcelona's kit in 1973 we also nicked Benfica's nickname. But before that we were the Glaziers, because our team was formed from the men who moved the actual crystal palace that housed the Great Exhibition of 1851 from Hyde Park to Penge. When new owners took us over in 2010, they offered fans a choice of four funky new badges to vote on for our funky new shirts. All the badges were simple variations of an eagle. Without a meeting, an email chain or a WhatsApp chat, fans unanimously decided none of them were any good. They wanted an eagle and a nod to our real past. The rather wonderful badge that adorns our kit now is a mighty eagle standing proudly on a palace of glass.

Shall I say it again? Kits matter. They even have their own nickname. Ask any Palace fan about the 'Brazil', the 'Virgin' or the 'Evil Slash' and you will be there for a long time.

And because kits matter, this book matters. I need to stop writing now because I could go on forever and that would leave Matt with fewer pages for his brilliant evocation of football kits from across the world. I know you will read this book with the same sound effects I did, a chorus of oohs and aahs at brilliant, and terrible, colour combinations and constant murmur of 'that's interesting' as Matt leads us through the glorious history of the football kits.

Two more thoughts to leave you with: I say 'probably' because as Matt will know, a definitive history of football kits is very tricky. It was a game played by mainly working-class men and clubs weren't expected to last for nearly 200 years and not a lot actually got written down in those days. And research for my own book indicates that much that did get into print was clearly written after a night in the pub.

And Matt was probably delighted that I acknowledged Aston Villa's part in my club's history. He may be less happy to know that I have a soft spot for Villa's deadly rivals, Birmingham City. Why? Because of their brilliant Belgian flag away kit of 1972.

Our football shirt stands as something to set our life's journey against

To the uninterested observer, my polyester polymer shirt is little more than an outrageously overpriced, queasy showcase for my expanding midlife midriff. But for me, my Villa kit is where the DNA of my long-suffering family and long-suffered club combine.

It has a badge of pride and despair, a colour scheme steeped in history that filters fellow fans as antagonists or acolytes. Without it, men would sheepishly struggle for stilted small talk on the weather or politics – subjects both boring and occasionally incendiary. Here, with your chemically created shirt, you have a conversational kickstarter or get out of jail free card.

Let's be honest, worn by anyone but a washboard-stomached athlete, football shirts are comically unflattering. Designed for a gazelle and often stretched over a warthog, they are stylish for the narrowest range of age and BMI. But, like a mediaeval court jester, they often give the wearer a free pass to look ridiculous (I see you, Tottenham's 2021 third kit).

Kit and Caboodle takes an unapologetically besotted look at how kits define us and message members of our tribe about the culture we advertise belonging to and the ones we fight against. Kits are lightning rods for the rise in consumerism, television paywalls, debt-laden leveraged buyouts and English football's Americanisation. Our shirts are often gaudy personal statements. This is me: this is my family, and this is my future. We wear a badge of honour, even if it is the crest of Stafford Rangers. We sing '(Exeter) City till I die' even if, over the last two decades, we already welcome the Grim Reaper's scythe by 4.30pm.

We also review some of the game's major narratives that are plotted through shirts, including the rise and mutation of gambling from pools to NFTs, attitudes to the LGBTQ+ community and how shirts serve as cultural signposts. Thankfully shorn of the violent overtones of the 1980s and my teenage years on Midlands terraces cut through with racist undercurrents, the stain of shame as I grew up wholeheartedly loving a sport drenched in misogyny and broiling anger has given way to a culture of joyous (if expensive) escapism. What other passion would prompt my line manager Dan to add to his work email yesterday, 'I miss being freezing cold at Exeter City'?

Liverpool University professor Rogan Taylor summed it up beautifully when describing his beloved Liverpool FC, 'Football is more than just a business. No one has their ashes scattered down the aisle at Tesco.'

Football kits also bring out our inner trainspotter. Inspired by the mighty Half Man Half Biscuit's 'All I Want for Christmas is a Dukla Prague Away Kit', quirky and left field kit choices scratch the trainspotter itch. When trawling through the Hope and Glory website for the Her Game Too merchandise they produced, I couldn't help being drawn by the home, away and training kit of the Falkland Islands. At half the price of a Premier League shirt and with the home kit boasting a ruby red sash, I just couldn't

stop myself. I justify it by saying how my uncle was on duty as part of the HMS *Endurance* crew when the Falklands War broke out in 1982, but I'm not fooling anyone. I also like to wear my Malawi Olympic football team shirt (a country I grew up in) to dip below the social radar unless — and this is one of the many joys of the kit — someone recognises it and initiates a convivial conversation.

Talking to Michael Maxwell from Football Shirt Collective, a group of over 20,000 lovers of 'vintage and modern classic shirts', he also shared how there is often a strong sense of rivalry within the shirt buying community:

'I would add that, from our perspective, we see the football kit community as growing at the moment. Especially post-Euro 2020, when people who never considered buying a football shirt (vintage or modern) bought one to follow England, people seem to be discussing football shirts and fandom around them much more. So while accounts/businesses like ours focus on the really fine details every day, bigger and more mainstream publications like The Athletic are also beginning to recognise this trend.

'From what we see and post, people just generally love looking at really nice football kits, and one level up from that is buying them, then collecting them, and eventually on to our stage of buying, selling and writing about them all day. That said, it can also be a flawed community at times — like any

> 'Football is more than just a business. No one has their ashes scattered down the aisle at Tesco.'

Liverpool University professor, Rogan Taylor

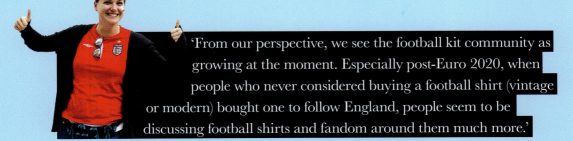

'From our perspective, we see the football kit community as growing at the moment. Especially post-Euro 2020, when people who never considered buying a football shirt (vintage or modern) bought one to follow England, people seem to be discussing football shirts and fandom around them much more.'

Michael Maxwell, Football Shirt Collective

sub-culture of football/sports fandom. This can arise from the issue of fakes on the market, or even just simple disagreements about how nice X's new home shirt is.'

My 16 years in Thailand saw some weird and not always wonderful kits that were a window on the kingdom's idiosyncratic football culture. With clubs often owned by political behemoths swimming in cash (including Buriram United with their identical stadium to Leicester's King Power), kits are often a platform to flex ministerial muscle. Beer shirt advertising is illegal, so Chang designed an identical logo for their water offering in a different colour. A very Thai solution. The Chiang Rai United kit is more billboard than shirt, but the Suphanburi FC design of 2015 is achingly stylish, especially when worn by a fan and lead singer of Thailand's favourite rock band, Toon from Bodyslam.

Kits are a joyous, infantilising dive into a culture of financial and social stupidity: a philosophy highly underrated in these dark times. It is a freeing state of mind that rejects the perceived wisdom of adulthood to escape doom-laden Covid death toll figures, baying mobs invading Capitol Hill or grim reports from Ukraine. The sheer scale of comment, reflection, social media-generated outrage by keyboard warriors in their mother's back bedroom and agent-manipulated transfer gossip creates a cacophony of white noise. The shirt is our cape of control and clarity.

Over the years, my Villa kit has made me proud (the 1982 European Cup Final win), depressed (the purgatorial 2015/16 season of not much more than a dozen points and a little over two dozen goals) or evangelical (when Villa's Covid-decimated boys' team with only five appearances between them, and those by Ben Chrisene playing for previous club Exeter City, held the mighty Liverpool for an hour in 2021). The shirt and game are the two tangible touchpoints that protect us from the onslaught of this unimaginably massive tide of distraction and, briefly, distil the game down into its constituent parts. They receive and hold the memories we will draw on into the future. Then it's back to the thumb-twiddling and social scrolling for a hit just not quite as sweet.

AUTHOR
Matt Riley

Too often this phrase is glossed over or considered the childish response of an emotionally stunted fan. But football goes DNA deep. Not only does it span family generations but, as real love should, motivates us to ridiculous flights of fancy.

Saturday, 25 September 2021's Aston Villa victory at Old Trafford, their first there since 2009, made any titbit of detail fair game. However poor the YouTube video or asinine the article, everything had to be hoovered up in a glorious day of freestyle emotional catharsis. As Kieran Maguire says in his and Kevin Day's imperious podcast *The Price of Football*, 'It is the first thing we think about when we wake up and the last thing we think about before we go to bed.' This sounds ridiculous only to those who can't feel real love because football love is the world's only limitless resource.

My all-consuming football affair does not mean I feel any less towards my wife or (occasionally) my sons.

It is not sordid (my wife noticed my profession of love on Facebook for Villa's keeper Emi Martínez and shrugged; it may have been a different reaction if that comment was directed at my next-door neighbour).

I love football

Former Women in Football CEO Jane Purdon describes the 'happy madness' football commands in the excellent anthology *Football, She Wrote*. Describing the moment in 1973 when the unfancied Sunderland scored against an imperious Leeds United in that season's FA Cup Final 33 minutes into the game, she said:

'Let me tell you how my seven-year-old heart experienced this. At 3.33pm and 50 seconds, I was a child who observed football with curiosity. Then, for a split second, there was just me and Ian Porterfield. Then he did this thing. And then I felt myself falling into a deep, deep pit. That pit was love. At 3.33pm and 52 seconds, my heart had gone forever. I was a football fan and a Sunderland fan.'[1]

Football love also allows us to keep a mistress. A lifelong Villa fan now living in Devon, I am a season ticket holder at Exeter City. It doesn't make me feel like a football swinger (Kevin Day may disagree), just a fan with lots of love (and frustration) to give. Most importantly in the context of this book, football love is not limited to who can feel it. On the terraces of my local Bangkok club and the away game Happy Bus where free rough-as-guts Leo beer provided by the club meant games were often hazy or non-recollections we were male, female, young, old, gay or straight but always Muang Thong United.

Working in a sensible and reliable job as the head of marketing and public relations for Harrow School Bangkok, I walked away from it to dive headfirst into the madness of Thai football. Financially ruinous but filled with lifelong memories, the whole experience had a heady and magnetic insanity that, six years later, is still slowly sinking in. The access it gave me to the powerbrokers with limitless funds was both intoxicating and occasionally terrifying. I wouldn't have changed a thing, even if my bank manager strongly disagrees.

My pay-the-bills job is as a lecturer in business management at Exeter University and I also volunteer for Exeter City. Oh, and I quite like football.

[1] Various authors, *Football, She Wrote: An Anthology of Women's Writing on the Game*, p172 (Floodlit Dreams, Kindle edition)

KIT & CABOODLE

Contents

Contents   15

01

We Wear Because We Care

QR you?

When we wear our club shirt we want to stand for something, whether it is our city (in the case of Forest Green Rovers a village) or the history of our club.

In Norway, Eliteserien club Tromsø released a third kit shirt that is a QR code. But, instead of it leading us to an 'engagement portal' with the club through a Wild West NFT (New Fleecing Tool) or cryptocurrency the kit leads, in collaboration with Amnesty International, to information about how the Qatari government are sportswashing, gender-washing and allegedly violating the norms of basic human

rights as they gear up to use our game as a fatuous exercise in sporting soft power. To add poetry to their point, the kit for the club promoted as champions of the Norwegian top flight last season uses the palette of the Qatari flag. Just when you think the Norwegians can't be any cooler, they inspire us again.

Tromsø are cut from a different cloth. Their mission is not to dominate Norwegian football (luckily as the nearest they have come to being champions is two runners-up spots in their 101 seasons) but to make a difference to their community and country. The four key points of their mission statement revolve around using football to improve public health, vague ambitions for their team to 'shape Norwegian top football', help youth players improve their skills and, 'contribute to activity, joy and meaning in developing and safe communities for all'. I think I feel another shirt purchase impulse developing.

Not surprisingly, the club promoted the kit as the first to incorporate a QR code and wore it on 12 December 2021 for their final game of the season, against Viking FK. Hashtag United might disagree. Their collector's edition home shirt for the 2021/22 season featured a QR code replacing the sponsor, giving fans access to exclusive content. But, considering Tromsø's QR destination, we can give them a free pass.

The only good news for the Qataris is that Tromsø have no chance of playing in the Champions League, so they won't need to see it beamed across global screens to remind people of the insidious process that led them to be awarded the world's biggest sporting tournament (something I had direct experience of when working for Thai club Muang Thong United after their game against a Qatari club in 2010). Talking to CNN, the club's managing director Øyvind Alapnes said,

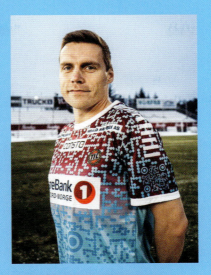

'We feel it is our duty to speak out. If we don't speak out with a loud voice for those who aren't heard, then who will do it?'

Chiming perfectly with football's attempts to support Ukraine and make football mean something, he added,

'Many people in football are seduced by money and just close their eyes to where the money comes from. Therefore, many don't risk standing up for something. We must dare to ask ourselves: Is it OK that someone dies in order for "my team" to be successful?'

And who better to model the new design than Malcolm Bidali? A former migrant worker arrested for daring to spotlight the working conditions of migrants through his blogs, he knows more than most the perils of being decent in a foetid environment. But he

The Norwegian national team, helped by the huge profile of their wunderkind Erling Haaland, warmed up with t-shirts demanding 'human rights on and off the pitch'.

is more than a figurehead to the club. A lengthy interview with him about his experiences figured prominently on the club website where he outlined the huge power imbalance between employers and employees in the Gulf state. The Kenyan, wearing the QR shirt, eloquently outlined how the 'kafala' system euphemistically described as a 'sponsorship' is little more than indentured servitude. As Bidali described it, 'The employer owns you.'

The club may have just over 9,000 Twitter followers, but a photo of the kit was proudly pinned to the top of their feed for weeks after their final game. Almost uniquely for the online world, the comments were wholly positive from fans across the globe asking how they could buy the design and the 4,000 likes were highly impressive for a club with a low international profile. For their 40,000 Facebook followers, the shirt was the page's profile picture until the start of the World Cup year. The club clearly doesn't do things by halves. Unfortunately, Tromsø would lose the game 2-0 and finish 12th in the 16-team league, but they sent a powerful message out that might is not always right.

This bright light of goodness in a dark World Cup world was supported by two sponsors of the Norwegian national team, who gave up their spots on the players' training kits in exchange for messages sharing alleged human rights abuses in Qatar. The national team, helped by the huge profile of their wunderkind Erling Haaland, also warmed up with t-shirts demanding 'human rights on and off the pitch'. With the match coming in the same week as the UN released their exhaustive Global Report on Corruption in Sport, the 300 pages included a single, woolly reference to human rights, describing how governments 'have the obligation to promote and protect human rights and to guarantee respect for the rule of law, including in the context of sports organizations'. Human rights lie at the heart of corruption. If the organisations who are supposed to be our leaders don't see it, then we have to lead the charge ourselves.

Of all the things we hold dear, it is our club shirt that weaves in the memories of our family history and serves as a signal to the world of what we, and our club, stand for. It is our true heritage. As Tromsø have shown, if we have enlightened custodians of our club or country, we can wear them with pride, not be forced to promote white-label, ghost ship companies making capital from catastrophe.

But more than that, Tromsø's stand invites us to confront and question what we believe in. Are we prepared to let actions we know are wrong simply slide by? Or, at personal cost, are we prepared

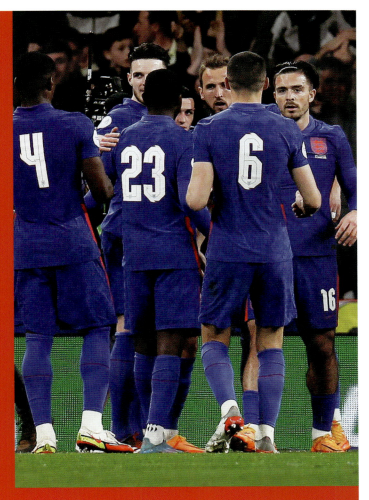

to say 'enough'? The shirts we wear and the messages they carry speak not only to who we choose (or are chosen) to support, but who we really are and what we stand for.

It's easy to forget that shirts can serve a higher purpose than setting us free from our money. For England's friendly against Switzerland on 27 March 2022, their shirts shone a light on dementia's cruel power to rob its victims of precious memories. After playing in standard shirts for the first half, they came out after the break wearing numbers but without names as a way of putting fans in the shoes of people trying to recall fast-fading facts and names of loved ones. The shirts were then auctioned to raise vital funds for Alzheimer's Society. This agreement with the FA and the charity runs for two years, and more of this innovative, thought-provoking and empathetic interaction will go a long way to ensuring people with the insidious condition are not forgotten.

Tromsø's QR shirt was a high-profile single-match tactic to support Amnesty, but there are longer-term partnerships and group efforts that cleanse the shirt of shady operators and make us proud to wear our colours again. The messages that shirts send can be subtle and heartfelt. For the 2022 season League of Ireland Premier Division side Shelbourne used their away shirt to recognise and commemorate their fans. The shirt's body weaves in the names of the 2021 season ticket holders as thanks for their

financial support during the pandemic and also weaves in the names of fans who have passed away during this terrible time.

When I talk about how football shirts can be used for good, I come back so often to German football. Marking over two years since full stadiums were allowed during the pandemic, when Dortmund played Leipzig in the Bundesliga on 2 April 2022 their shirt featured the names of all 978 official fan clubs spelling out 'Danke'. Such a simple, heartfelt and powerful gesture shows how meaningful a shirt's message can be when it is an example of enlightened self-interest.

During their friendly against Switzerland on 27 March 2022, England's shirts had no player names printed on the back, symbolising dementia's cruel power to rob its victims of precious memories.

On Saturday, 5 March 2022, in front of a record 74,479 fans at Bank of America Stadium, Charlotte FC played their first home game in Major League Soccer against Los Angeles Galaxy. Although Galaxy would shave the win with the only goal, the game was the setting for the kind of shirt story we all need to hear in these dark times.

In 2010 Galaxy's Sacha Kljestan (then playing for the now-defunct Chivas USA) visited a cancer patient at Children's Hospital Los Angeles and gave a young fan a jersey. In December 2009, the then-seven-year-old Chris Hegardt was hospitalised after being struck in the stomach with a ball when playing in a tournament. The ball ruptured a tumour on his liver, requiring emergency surgery. A biopsy later revealed that Hegardt had malignant cancer covering a third of his liver. He went through six rounds of chemotherapy and a liver transplant. Now, a dozen years later, that young fan is a 20-year-old professional player. Hegardt plays in midfield for Charlotte FC.

The day before the game, Kljestan tweeted:

Sacha Kljestan ✔
@SachaKljestan

My wife and I visited this young man back in 2010 at Children's Hospital LA. Today I ran into his parents in our hotel lobby in Charlotte. His name is Chris Hegardt and he's a rookie midfielder for @CharlotteFC. I gave him a jersey once, hopefully he will give me his tomorrow'

Following Galaxy's win, the two met on the field and did a jersey swap a decade in the making. Although neither player started, they both came on as second-half subs and for a few minutes were on the field together. Damn those onions.

During the Russian invasion of Ukraine in February 2022, 2. Bundesliga club Schalke removed the Russian Gazprom logo from team shirts and replaced it with 'Schalke 04'. German newspaper *Bild* pre-empted the move by transposing the message 'Freedom to Ukraine' on to any images of Schalke's previous shirts as soon as the invasion was announced. Wolfsburg also swapped the shirt sponsor for their game on 5 March against Union Berlin from VW to a peace logo. Köln went a step further against Hoffenheim the same day. Replacing the Rewe logo on the front with 'Stop War', and the Devk sleeve logo with the peace symbol, the game's corner flags were also the colours of Ukraine, the pylons of the RheinEnergieStadion were lit up in blue and yellow before these one-off shirts were then auctioned to support Ukrainian victims of the Russian invasion. These were just some of the German clubs who decided that this was the time for solidarity over commerce. This type of swift and heartfelt decision to support an attacked country seems to fit effortlessly with the German 50 plus one ownership model, where supporters can drive values as a communal return on investment.

Shirts are a nimble and highly visible way to send a message of defiance and support. West Ham players warmed up for their game against Wolves on 27 February 2022, wearing Andriy Yarmolenko's number seven shirt after he was given compassionate leave, and Wolves wore 'No To War' shirts. But, although Premier League matches showed their support for Ukraine with scarves, flags, bouquets and captains' armbands, the shirts remained largely unaltered. This was an opportunity missed to generate even more money to support stricken Ukrainians, show how shirts can send out messages of solidarity and make it even harder for Russian and Chinese video editors to cut out any references to the 'military operation' in their highlights packages. By the end of March, England had decided to give their captain an armband in Ukrainian colours for the games against Switzerland and Ivory Coast at Wembley, while Ukraine flags were flying over their training pitch at St George's Park as they prepared for these games.

Danish Superliga side Brøndby wore a special tribute kit to show solidarity with Ukraine the same week, inverting their usual shirt and shorts colours to resemble Ukraine's flag. After their game against SønderjyskE the shirts were auctioned, with all the money raised sent to help Ukrainian children suffering during the war. Adding to this, on 1 March, Adidas suspended their deal to make Russian kits for both the men's and women's national teams, an agreement that had been in place since 2009. To be fair to Premier League clubs, Manchester United would also announce the termination of their long-term relationship with Russian airline Aeroflot on the same day as Schalke's decision, cancelling a deal that had been extended in 2017 for £40m.

Other clubs activated their kits to show solidarity with the besieged country. The coolest tribute to the fallen of Ukraine was made by Italian Serie C side Carrarese. Their one-off shirt worn on Saturday, 12 March against Modena was an *Escape to Victory* tribute. Sales of the shirt went to support the work of Medicins Sans Frontieres in Ukraine.

The design is achingly attractive and touches a nerve with its theme of trying to escape a tyrant. I really need to lock my credit card away.

Some English clubs did make decisions about wearing kits to give support. Brighton committed to wearing their yellow and blue kits in early March 2022 against Newcastle and Aston Villa. The sheer magnitude of the horror has spiked the guns of keyboard warriors who would cry foul 'virtue signalling' and shows the incredible power a shirt's colour can convey. Even my doorstep club Exmouth Town wearing their yellow and blue kit for the rest of the season gives a chance to do something rather than nothing at a time when we all feel powerless, helpless and hopeless. And, despite the caution for Villa's Matty Cash after taking off his shirt to reveal a message of support for Polish international team-mate and Dynamo Kyiv player Tomasz Kędziora after scoring for Villa against Brighton, the Premier League decided players would be allowed to protest the war in Ukraine without fear of punishment, so long as displays were not offensive.

Ever-stylish AC Milan chose to raise vital funds for Ukraine by producing a shirt inspired by former striker Andriy Shevchenko's 2003 Champions League Final kit with a timely twist by incorporating the Ukrainian flag on its shoulders and 'AC Milan for peace' on the front. On the back was Shevchenko's name and his iconic number seven. Shirts were offered at a cut-price €50 (£41) from the club website and all the money went to the Italian Red Cross and their project in Ukraine. The inspiration came after Shevchenko, who coached Ukraine at Euro 2020, tearfully addressed Italian TV, sharing his fears for his family's safety and begging for international support for his embattled nation.

USL League One club Forward Madison also released their tribute to the brave Ukrainians on 8 April when the Wisconsinites released a shirt designed in Ukraine's colours and wore it the following day for their first home game of the season against Union Omaha. All proceeds would go to UNICEF for Ukrainian relief, shirt sponsors Dairyland Insurance and Just Coffee Cooperative stepped aside to be replaced by 'United for Ukraine' and kit manufacturers Hummel donated their income from the new kit to the Red Cross. There was also the heartening replacement of the sleeve sponsor with a vibrant sunflower to showcase a popular Ukrainian national symbol. This was a theme elegantly picked up by J.League side Shonan Bellmare, using Ukraine's flag as their colour palette and a deeply moving image on the base of the shirts' back showing Ukrainian children holding up the flowers in a kit known as the 'sunflower uniform'.

As Forward Madison shared so eloquently on their website:

'Our club best expresses its voice through kits and it was clear that our best way to raise money for Ukrainian relief was through a unique kit. We were able to work with our designers and suppliers to quickly develop a unique kit. We feel that this was the best way for our club to have a small impact on the relief efforts.'

Although pricey at $90 (£69), signed game-worn shirts were also made available through online auction and the club set no end date for the shirt sales.

But the best people to wear shirts in support of the besieged Ukrainians were the country's biggest team, Shakhtar Donetsk. The 2009 UEFA Cup winners started their 'Football for Peace' tour in Greece against league leaders Olympiakos on 9 April. Each Shakhtar outfield player wore a shirt with the name of one of their ten besieged cities in place of their own. Movingly, 176 toys were also placed in the stadium seats to commemorate the children murdered since the conflict began on 24 February. Talking to the BBC, Shakhtar Donetsk's CEO Sergei Palkin said:

'We want to talk about war and peace in Ukraine in these matches. The need to end this madness and return to normal life and to rebuild the country.'

Shakhtar went on to play Fenerbahçe, Hajduk Split and Lechia Gdańsk, with other opponents likely to be added by the time you read this. All gate receipts were donated to humanitarian aid for Ukraine, while toys were also collected for refugee children and a moment's silence was held to honour those killed in the conflict. Shirts can be a catalyst for kindness and shared humanity. Shakhtar would lose the game by a single goal, but their bigger aim was achieved with dignity and defiance.

It's not only what people have worn to support Ukraine, but what they will no longer be seen in. On 2 March Everton decided to sever all ties with Russian companies USM, Megafon and Yota with immediate effect. Megafon were taken off as the main sponsor of the women's team shirts. Indirectly, via their ownership by the sanctioned Russian Roman Abramovich, Chelsea were given a last-minute kit headache for their game against Norwich on 10 March. The main shirt sponsors 3 made it clear that they no longer wanted to be associated with the club or kit. Luckily for Chelsea (and unluckily for the Norwich Sports Direct store), 3 agreed on a brief stay of execution. Bizarrely, despite pre-match shirt graphics for their next game against Newcastle being sponsorless, they would take to the field with the logo still there. Maybe the cost of buying new shirts with frozen credit cards was just too much.

In July 2019, second-tier Australian club Wollongong Wolves wore a thought-provoking home shirt paying tribute, in partnership with local artist Trent Duff, to National Aborigines and Islanders Day. The design showcased imagery from the local Illawarra tribe working closely with the Illawarra Local Aboriginal Land Council and the Wreck Bay Sharks to honour indigenous culture and promote opportunities for local indigenous footballers. They may be a small club, but they showed a big heart and helped to weaponise kindness. My credit card is buckling under the strain.

Aston Villa started a partnership in 2006 with Acorns, a hospice for terminally ill children, but it was when they became shirt sponsors between 2008 and 2010 that the connection kicked into a higher gear, one that many Villans look wistfully back to as they explore their latest shirts promoting gambling and selling second-hand cars. Villa's shirt relationship echoed Barcelona's commitment to UNICEF. Shirts mostly shout at us to consume but Barcelona's half-decade UNICEF partnership shows they can also give us cause to pause. Serially successful Manchester City CEO Ferran Soriano describes in his thought-provoking book *Goal: The Ball Doesn't Go in by Chance* how, when he was vice-president of Barcelona, they not only chose to reject shirt sponsor income but gave an annual €1.5m to the charity. Soriano went on to explain:

'The strategy was a short- to mid-term one, risky and not so easy to implement. In the short term, it meant giving up the €20m every year from the internet betting company bwin [which ended up on Real Madrid's jersey] and, instead, donating €1.5m to UNICEF every year. But the strategy fitted nicely with the spirit of the club that we wished to project worldwide.'[2]

[2] Soriano, F., *Goal: The Ball Doesn't Go in by Chance*, p68-69 (Palgrave Macmillan UK, Kindle edition)

This partnership was not purely a charitable gift. It underpinned a huge rise in the global Barcelona fanbase through their 'brand synergy' which led to a sharp spike in club earnings and the price of a post-UNICEF shirt slot was also handsomely enhanced, but seeing reputational sincerity over tawdry damage is always a heartwarming chance to give cheer. This universally respected partner was the ideal delivery system for the club ethos of being *más que un club* (more than a club) and allowed Barça to have a unified vision, in the eyes of its global fanbase at least, that started with the shirt and spread out through the whole organisation. Of course, that moment of pride was to be swept away in 2010 when the antithesis of everything UNICEF stands for paid €30m a season. The Qatar Foundation is, just like Newcastle's owners, totally independent of the Qatari state and would never sponsor a club for any other reason than to make the game better for fans of every orientation.

Barcelona's shirt messaging in February 2022 by the men's and women's teams was to celebrate the Lunar New Year. Large patches on their left sleeves used Chinese characters and a tiger image for their games against Atlético Madrid and Eibar respectively. Despite the vast amount of Barcelona fakes on open display, south and east Asia remain a clear target for the Catalans, where marketing campaigns are coordinated through the office in Hong Kong, which opened in 2013. This decision to get Spanish feet on the ground in key markets has clearly worked, with Barça being voted best online club in China for 2020 and 2021 by sports marketing agency Mailman.

Whether this strategy can translate into increased legitimate shirt sales for markets with a relatively low GDP and high shirt prices remains to be seen. For example,

at one of Thailand's most popular football stores, Ari, in downtown Bangkok, a Thai League 1 shirt for 2021 champions BG Pathum United will cost you 1,099 Baht (£24.50) but a shirt from 2021 Premier League champions Manchester City will set you back 3,000 Baht (£67.00). If you wanted a Liverpool shirt, that figure rises to an eye-watering £102.00 for a country where the minimum wage – often ignored – is set at £6.00 a day. It's no wonder that the huge labyrinth of fake shirt sellers based around the National Stadium BTS skytrain station do a roaring trade.

Closer to home, Covid-19 has given clubs the chance to show their appreciation of the NHS and the members of our society left behind as a wedge is driven between the haves and have nots during this interminable pandemic. In 2020 Brighton and Hibs used their shirts to thank our NHS heroes on the front line and Albion also thanked key workers on the sleeve. Money raised from sales made up part of the Seagulls' Albion as One campaign which players launched and added to from their wages for funds to

be distributed to local Sussex charities crumpling under the weight of the pandemic. Hibernian took a more direct route. Their 'Thank You NHS' shirt message had, by Christmas 2021, raised £40,000 directly to the local Edinburgh and Lothians Health Foundation. The shirts were the centrepiece for a range of initiatives including all profits from those buying the special edition shirts, the money raised by cardboard cutouts of supporters during the fanless football period, auctioning the shirt, revenue from selling Covid masks and a heartening range of other activities for, let's not forget, a club struggling massively themselves. In the 2018/19 season before Covid struck they lost three-quarters of a million pounds (although that's peanuts compared to the £943,076 Chelsea lost each week during Abramovich's 19-year reign) and were rescued by the sale of John McGinn to Aston Villa for the absolute bargain for Villa but a lifesaver for Hibs of £2.79m.

There was also a collective response by the Premier League with the inclusion of blue hearts for the NHS in the middle of shirt fronts with Black Lives Matter on the right sleeves from June 2020 until the end of that season. For the first game of Project Restart players would have the equality slogan on their backs in place of their names to give the campaign strong profile and momentum. These were widely praised initiatives, which made the Premier League's refusal to support homeless charity Shelter on Boxing Day 2021 seem churlish and contrarian.

A collective response from the Premier League saw the inclusion of blue hearts for the NHS in the middle of shirt fronts with Black Lives Matter on the right sleeves from June 2020 until the end of that season.

Peter Crouch, in his role as Dulwich Hamlet director (and their former player), modelled their shirt featuring the charity's logo which they would wear over the festive season in their game against Welling United and then auction off the 19 shirts for further funds to support them. In an endearing extra flourish, the successful bidders were presented with their shirt by one of the starting line-up and substitutes from that match. They probably missed a trick by not making any available for sale with the attention Crouch brought to the project, but it was a heartfelt and admirable gesture.

The EFL were also happy to oblige and took full part in the Sky Sports campaign, but it was left to five Premier League clubs to break the rules and support it. Brentford, Brighton (not surprisingly after seeing their coach Graham Potter spend a night on the streets to show his support), Everton, Tottenham and Watford broke ranks. Goalkeepers also tried to show their support independently by challenging each other to choose their away tops. M22.1 of the rulebooks must never be broken, it seems, making the naysayers look out of touch with the game they are supposed to be stewards of.

Harry Kane is magic

Luckily, some Premier League stars had already taken things into their own hands to show how shirts can be a force for good. This was also something my favourite podcasters chose to support. Kevin Day and Kieran Maguire's (at the time of writing) BAFTA-repelling podcast *The Price of Football* launched a competition in late March 2022 to design and produce two sets of kits for donation to a grassroots club chosen by their global audience. Giving a nod to Kieran's colour blindness and advocacy of a condition affecting almost one in ten of the population, they chose white as the base, a crest featuring the presenters' pets flanking a shield and a motto riffing on Kieran's love of forensic accounting, 'In Veritas Amortisi.'

The two men's volcanic excitement at being part of a kit design process shows just how much emotion is woven into the fabric of our shirts and helped move Kevin one step nearer to the fever dream he mentioned in the foreword of returning his beloved Palace's kit to claret and blue on his first day in charge as owner.

In their hermetically sealed world of weekly million-pound income, it's tempting to conclude that Premier League footballers exist as a closed-shop group of small corporations circling each other in perpetual wage and sponsorship escalation. But sometimes stories show they know how lucky they are to inhabit this rarefied universe and understand this destination couldn't have happened without help on the journey.

Talking to Sky Sports in the summer of 2020, England captain Harry Kane enthused over his 'magic partnership' with League Two strugglers Leyton Orient. Kane was surprised and delighted with the spike in shirt sales for the O's driven by his gesture. By 1 June 2020, Orient had overtaken shirt sales for the previous season by 25 per cent and had orders coming in from 31 countries including Mexico, Russia and New Zealand. Kane told Sky:

'It's a great surprise and hopefully, they continue to sell that many shirts because I know the charities will really benefit from the ten per cent they're getting as well. They'll use that money to great effect.'

In lovethesales.com's league table of shirt sales published in August 2021, Orient were placed in a healthy 42nd place, one ahead of Portsmouth and just behind Bolton and Blackburn in this 92-team league and had leapt a huge 35 places from the season before. There seems to be a Kane bounce happening at the online tills. So pleased was Kane that on 6 May 2021, he extended his shirt sponsorship agreement, a hat tip to the club that helped form his career when a young Harry went on the first of his four loans from Spurs in 2011. The shirt space isn't used to lionise his brand further (which wouldn't be a great marketing ploy choosing a club that managed to struggle to an 11th-placed finish in the fourth tier in 2021 and were in a similar situation the following season). Instead, he has given the platform to three worthy causes who need it far more than him. That season the home shirt paid homage to the NHS heroes and heroines who saved us from further deaths during the pandemic. The 2021/22 shirt promoted Tommy Club, which is run by the Royal British Legion to support the country's most vulnerable armed forces veterans and the away shirt continued to promote the Essex-based Haven House Children's Hospice which provides free care to life-limited children and their families. The third kit promoted the mental health charity Mind.

Kane also sponsors the women's team as they look to move through the divisions after a challenging

relationship with the club. Like Juan Mata and his Common Goal scheme, which aims to persuade other highly paid stars to donate one per cent of their wages to charity, Kane is using his fame to enrich his legacy and respect within the game instead of yet another product-placed photoshoot, gaudy and oversized watch or ghost-written autobiography. On 23 September 2021, Orient's highly respected former CEO Danny Macklin was bursting with pride to share on Twitter how the project had won Partnership of the Year at the Football Business Awards for the second time:

'The teamwork that has gone into this has been rewarded. HUGE plaudits to Josh, Pa, Emily, Lucy, Lucy, Jake, Anna, Luke and Dan plus many others plus huge thanks above all else to @ HKane @ck66ltd and their team.'

As we stumble out of a bleak lockdown period into a war in Europe, this is the culture that needs to be championed. Ronaldo might have 20 supercars and Neymar travels in a £6m private jet, but their story is pure Kardashian. Clearly Kane is also a multi-millionaire, but he wears the role with more humility and relatability. Neymar lobbied to leave Barcelona because his ego couldn't deal with a role as Lionel Messi's understudy (a view he may have reconsidered when they became team-mates again in Paris). Kane has been a Spurs player man and boy for 17 years and counting.

But wearing because we care doesn't need to have a charity sponsor it. Football Shirts For Charity was set up by Tania Harding and Jayme Sporton to support three worthy charities in the Bobby Moore Fund, Cancer Research and Sebastian's Action Trust (a home for terminally ill children). Both founders carry harrowing cancer stories of people close to them and their project relies on shirt donations which are then sold and the profits shared among the three charities. It is also great to report that the winner of the 2021 Football Shirt Charity Run was my local team Exeter City. They contributed 27 shirts to top the 53-team table, collecting more points than Leeds, Aston Villa and Arsenal combined (a sentence I will never type again). Of the many inspiring initiatives that show how our shirts carry our life stories is #ShirtStorySunday where followers share the stories of shirts that mean so much to them. For Sharon Zoomer, her Manchester United shirt brought back the fascination of watching Eric Cantona – upturned collar and in his pomp – when she was living in Holland during the 1995/96 Premier League season. For Sharon, kits can help us express ourselves and build our confidence. After swapping shirts with former United player Robin van Persie, she shared:

'I think his move from Arsenal to United sums up how I feel about collecting: do what feels good to YOU to get the best out of yourself.'

Despite a Liverpool and Manchester United family background, Josh Spoychalski fell in love with a Norwich City shirt found at the bottom of a pile from across the globe and it fuelled his love of collecting shirts to immerse himself in the stories they told. For some, the shirt shows a higher purpose. Callum Thompson's AFC Yorkies kit tells the story of why this charity team from Hull means so much to him. From the 'red threads that signify unity and friendship' to a crest that celebrates the Yorkshire regiment's connections to many of the current and former players, his shirt is a constant reminder of why he plays the game and how important it is for him, his team-mates and the Hull community. The power of a crest design to act as a call to arms was also taken up by Her Game Too partners Rochdale AFC. In March 2022 they redesigned it to include the logo of a campaign fighting relentlessly for the respect and acceptance that women deserve in the football world.

My shirt stories

We lived in Thailand for 16 years and I worked for two of the biggest clubs in the kingdom. I shared a Suphanburi FC shirt with a representative of Yokohama F. Marinos after we had signed a partnership agreement. Not only do I love its design, but it reminds me of how shirts can represent everything a club stands for and what it hopes to achieve. It's also a great way to forge friendships. Connections like these become a shorthand for both sides in an agreement buying into what each other stands for in a more meaningful way than poring over a memorandum of understanding or a kitsch dry ice laser show.

The business and football connections forged by this agreement all had this one moment of shared values through shirts at its core and always reminds me of the power a shirt projects to effect meaningful change through creating connections and crossing boundaries. Even though each club was vastly different in size and scope, there was a feeling of real respect and empathy when we held our shirt together in Bangkok's palatial Paragon Exhibition Centre.

The 'f' in family

Now we are back in England doing standard jobs, memories of working in Thai football get rosier by the year. At our local Bangkok team Muang Thong United there were plenty of characters and Noi (meaning 'small' in Thai) was one of them. His whole life revolved around the club (and Phuket FC whose green shirt he was wearing was also owned by the club). Even though to my wife it was a harder sell than a weekend in Wuhan, it also gave me an occasional chance to bring my family to matches. The kids were keen to wear the home and away shirts but my better 80 per cent was a tougher nut to crack. The rough-as-guts Leo beer brings back memories of matches becoming increasingly surreal and, despite the large majority of the crowd being under the spell of the beer Chang

don't like to export, there was rarely any trouble. When it did happen, it was more driven by politics than lager. Seeing those shirts worn by Josh, Ollie, Noi and I remind me of simpler times when our shirts made us part of a Thai community that welcomed us with open arms and crates of beer.

Our Zoe

Some days you just have to jump all over because, for reasons you don't fully understand, everything good you have worked for comes together and peaks at the same time. It's 17 October 2021, and my local club have put together a Her Game Too weekend with the men on Saturday and the women playing the day after. My wife and I sponsor one of the women's team. Zoe Watkins not only scored the equaliser in front of a record crowd of 1,372 but slotted a penalty that helped City beat arch-rivals Plymouth Argyle in a cup match played at St James Park. In the club bar afterwards, the old-style City shirt I wore, and Zoe's latest edition were two elements in a room pulsating with pure joy and flowing with Thatchers Cider. Our shirts were the focus point for years of trying to help the club, support both the men's and women's teams and volunteer for them. It's rare for life to conjure up pure magic in a single afternoon, but when it happens it takes on a momentum all its own and the ride is life-affirming.

The Three Amigos

As my sons grow older and my role moves from being a caregiver to a 24-hour ATM, some photos remind me of days when sharing the same shirt and going to the match made them excited. This was during my time as English media officer at provincial Bangkok club Suphanburi FC. They didn't know it at the time, but having security passes and access to the players and president was something they wouldn't experience again but the warning signs are flashing. Watery smiles betray their slow realisation that my football day started at the team hotel hours before kick-off, was punctuated by long-dead hours waiting for the next stage in the matchday routine, involved squinting at the game from the media room in the corner of the stadium and wouldn't end until the press conference and late-night meal with staff had finished before it was time to record the English highlights commentary. One saving grace for me was they had yet to find their beer drinking feet. Otherwise, I would have been jettisoned as soon as the stadium bar opened and until their money ran out.

Through the Football Shirts For Charity website (footballshirtsfc.co.uk) Jayme and Tania continue to receive donations, sell retro vintage football shirts and hold events such as the #FootballShirtCharity5K knowing that 'Shirts Hold The Memories' and provide a catalyst for doing great charitable work.

Messages
in Black
and White

Choosing to produce a black kit can have a benign message. Real Madrid's offering introduced for *El Clásico* on 20 March 2022 drew howls of online outrage (no, honestly) as it meant both clubs chose to play in away kits.

Barça were celebrating their Catalan heritage and Madrid's black, in another collaboration with Adidas designer Yohji Yamamoto, celebrated the club's 120th anniversary. But black shirts also create a canvas for more powerful messages.

On 15 January 2022 Doncaster Rovers lost 2-1 at home to Wigan. There were just over 7,000 fans at the Eco-Power Stadium and little national profile, but the club needed to act after the grandson of former Rovers player Dave Miller, James, took his own life. Doncaster would finish the afternoon rooted to the bottom of the League One table but they chose to use the game and their kits to shine a light on those of us struggling with the 'black dog' of poor mental health. The whole kit was black, with only the player numbers and EFL logos deviating from the theme. The club sponsor LNER (London North Eastern Railway) had already stepped aside as shirt sponsor for this

third kit when it was launched in late November 2021, giving the space to mental health campaigners CALM (Campaign Against Living Miserably). The kit message is that those struggling with their mental health are fighting a battle often invisible to others. For every shirt sold, £5 was donated to CALM and this kit was worn throughout the season to keep the narrative going. Online accusations of being 'political' and of gaslighting show that the campaign is working as this hollow anger only gets the message of a hidden scourge accentuated by lockdowns into more conversations. Doncaster may be small in size and scope, but they have the power of purpose to drive them on.

In late January 2022, the sumptuous and deeply researched *These Football Times* partnered with custom kit designers Icarus to release the Blackout Kit V1 which would help raise funds for Football Beyond Borders, a group that, 'Works with young people from disadvantaged backgrounds who are disengaged at school, helping them finish school with the skills and grades to make a successful transition into adulthood.

We do this by providing long-term, intensive support, built around relationships and young people's passions, in the classroom and beyond.' The kit design creates a quiet and reflective template that has small detailing of *These Football Times* on the collar and a black crest. Stylish, empowering and inclusive, it infuses consumerism with meaning, rejecting the billboardisation of our beloved shirts to make a bold statement of who we are and what we stand for. Later that month, reporter Trevor Murray spoke to Icarus's founder Robby Smukler about the pull of a football shirt and the messages it transmits about who we are and what we stand for.

of our society. The hashtag was also written in rainbow colours across the back of the shirt's neck. After playing on 19 March against FC Zürich, the shirts were auctioned to support Ukrainian refugees taking shelter in European countries.

Values-driven kit manufacturer Jark, one of the official apparel partners of Her Game Too, also released a range of merchandise to help raise mental health awareness in early 2022. Half of the purchase price went to the Bobby Copping Foundation, named after a player forced to retire through a head injury at the heartbreakingly early age of 19, 'To help us educate young sportsmen and women about

'Football shirts give off a lot of signals,' Robby Smukler said. 'They can indicate what you're passionate about, where you're from, and even your politics in some cases. That's part of what makes them so special as a piece of clothing – there's really so much that's tied into a football shirt.'

Smukler's view was beautifully illustrated in late March 2022 when Swiss Super League side BSC Young Boys released a limited-edition #YBFOREVERYONE shirt that supported a week dedicated to the fight against racism in the club's home city of Bern. The black jersey base was complemented by rainbow pinstripes to highlight how a fight against racism is also a step towards making all forms of equality, diversity and inclusion part

the perils of elite sport when it all comes crashing down.' The football shirt is also in black, reflecting Bobby 'finding myself in some very dark places at times'. There is something incredibly energising about making us consumers who make a difference. Not to the owner of a club who took control through a highly debt-fuelled leveraged buyout, but to people who need our help and find solace and strength in our purchase decision.

No More Red

Following in Tromsø's footsteps on 7 January 2022, Arsenal launched an incredibly thought-provoking and timely campaign through their sponsors Adidas. After a heartbreaking 10,000 knife crimes in London between June 2020 and June 2021 and a record number of teenagers murdered by stabbing in the capital, Arsenal's current and former players joined famous fans to front a highly evocative and energising short video to explain their campaign and the need for it. Idris Elba, Ian Wright and players Emile Smith Rowe and Bukayo Saka shared their manifesto for change.

Walking around the Emirates, Elba kicked the video off by reminding us that 'our future stars live yards from this stadium', supported by Gooners legend Wright adding, 'They look to this place, as we all do, for inspiration.' For Elba, 'It's getting harder to see, though. They're looking elsewhere. They're looking over their shoulder. There's blades, there's beef. It's madness. These kids are killing their future.' Smith Rowe challenges us by asking, 'How do we change this?' and Saka appeals to us through the power of football to 'change our lives'. Ian Wright spotlights how for fans, the players wear 'the colours they love. Let's use them' before all the video's voices conclude with its key mantra of 'no more red'.

In his pre-match press conference, Arsenal manager Mikel Arteta, appropriately dressed in white, gave his wholehearted support to the initiative and why it was important for his club to make a strong statement about knife crime:

'We have the capacity to give exposure to that issue in London and everyone at the club has been extremely supportive, starting with the players and our sponsors; especially Adidas which has been exceptionally good to come with some great ideas to support that.'

But Arteta went on to address the issue that some people may feel this shirt was no more than an ephemeral publicity stunt to this perceptive reporter's question, 'There's lots of proud Arsenal fans but there are some Arsenal fans who are thinking beyond Sunday. What will the players do? What will the club do? How will you keep pushing this issue forward and keep highlighting serious youth violence in the capital?'

Arteta responded:

'There is a lot of work that is done outside the lights obviously and a lot of people that have spent a lot of effort to try to design different ways and ideas to support that cause. It is not something that is going to be resolved overnight but certainly, given the exposure and attention that is needed and hopefully many other people can jump on this initiative and try to resolve it because it's a big issue in London.'

The FA Cup tie at Nottingham Forest being shown on terrestrial ITV instead of behind a paywall gave the campaign a huge platform and the pre-match support went a long way to giving it another profile spike.

In the build-up, Idris Elba joined Mark Pougatch, Roy Keane and Ian Wright pitchside in his white shirt to passionately describe why the campaign was so important. Frustratingly for the keyboard warriors, he wasn't wearing it because he was a big Hollywood star but as the head of one of the ten community action groups, Don't Stab Your Future, trying to fight the deadly wave of senseless killing.

'We all watched football as kids, and it spoke to us. So, we're using the innovation, the partnership to say, "Hey guys, how can we make a stand against knife crime?"' the actor said.

Wright went on to identify the sweeping cuts to community services and open spaces to let off steam and be counselled before making poor decisions that have underscored this bleak scenario:

'In the last ten years 750 youth centres closed down, 4,500 youth workers out of work. People that you build relationships with, people that know you.'

Elba eloquently and passionately argued his case, even disarming Keane. Clear, simple and articulate, his argument also touched on the way brands and shirts can lead the conversation moving forward when he highlighted the future potential of similar campaigns doing good work with 'innovation between brands like football and clothing'.

At kick-off, as the Gunners entered the field wearing white shirts in the FA Cup third round for the first time since a 1970 replay defeat to Blackpool, the video had been viewed an astonishing quarter of a million times. You'll be shocked to learn how the new kit received plenty of online moral outrage. The first response was the usual brainless rant from people rushing to apoplexy before reading the message's content. The club are changing their kit yet again (they aren't), and this is just another ridiculously expensive cash grab (it isn't). Some were dismissive of the whole campaign because the white was too close to the hated kit of rivals Spurs. Others said it was no more than fatuous gaslighting that would achieve nothing on London's dangerous streets. They could have a point but, given the choice between doing something or nothing, surely it is better to try and fail instead of throwing our hands up in despair. But there were also some more nuanced responses. One was from @joe_gresty on Twitter:

Joe Gresty
@joe_gresty

This is a really important message. One of the ways Glasgow reduced its knife crime was getting the message out at the grassroots level, into schools. A club like Arsenal putting this out is huge even if it gets the message across to a small per cent.

Another addressed the issue of fakes. We all knew that, at kick-off, there were already thousands of knock-off copies ready for distribution around the world, but what will that say about those who choose to buy them? It is easy to be dismissive of what looks like another shirt gimmick to boost sales and create extra planned obsolescence, but this campaign is different. The shirts could not be bought but would be offered for free to people creating positive change in the local communities around the Emirates. Or, as the Arsenal Twitter feed challenged its 18 million followers:

Arsenal FC
@Arsenal

You can't buy these shirts; you earn them by doing positive things.

As the shirts were strictly limited to people making a meaningful difference to the safety of lives on the streets in north London, someone in Truro or Falkirk would immediately be identified as a wearer of a fake. With sad predictability, eBay was peppered with 'brand new with tags' white shirts as people tried to cash in on the lack of supply and heightened demand. By April there was allegedly a Gabriel Martinelli match-worn shirt on offer for a mere £585. As bidding was about to start it was mysteriously withdrawn. I can only hope this was driven by a pang of conscience.

There were even people trying to exploit Leeds United's Her Game Too match against Manchester United on Sunday, 20 February 2022 by selling unofficial versions of the tops the Yorkshire club's players wore in the warm-up to celebrate their new partnership with the campaign. Proceeds from official merchandise go to supporting grassroots development of the women's game, so these people trying to turn a quick profit were ignoring and disrespecting the ethics of a group of women trying to make a positive difference. Normally it wouldn't matter but for the Arsenal campaign, they will also be indulging in Stolen Valour. It is not a valid defence to say you always buy the latest shirt or that you are a huge fan. By wearing this shirt, you are passing yourself off as something you are not. Will they be bothered? Probably not, but by refusing to sell copies, Adidas has cleverly turned the tables on those who see fakes as fair game. When the original is ridiculously expensive consumers have a point, but when it is free and has to be earned, they just make themselves look as inauthentic as the shirts they are wearing.

This is a tremendously powerful image of the red of Arsenal running through their fans' veins and the red blood being spilt needlessly in the stadium's surrounding streets. The power of the shirt is the perfect catalyst for these two striking images. The draining of the shirt's font and the barely visible logos of the club and sponsors creates a feeling of calm reflection as the normal hectoring demands to consume (while visiting

Rwanda) fall silent for an hour and a half. It's also really pleasing to see that, although in a muted colour scheme, the right sleeve has been given over to No More Red.

The game at Forest on 9 January 2022 was the campaign's centrepiece. Whether by happy accident or design, these were the best possible opponents to share their message with. Three Forest players moved to play for Dial Square FC (Arsenal's original name) in 1886 and had taken their red Forest kits with them. Forest being formed the year before, they already had their club colours selected and having such limited funds available to launch a new kit, the Londoners decided the cheapest option was to dress the rest of the team in the same colour as the new recruits and the knitting needles went into overdrive. The 2022 meeting created perfect symmetry.

After the game, the match-worn outfield shirts were presented to the other nine organisations working in the local areas specifically trying to repel the rising tide of pointless murder including the Stephen Lawrence Day Foundation, Steel Warriors and Box Up Crime. The next steps were the creation of safe spaces to play football and No More Red mentoring schemes where young people doing positive work in the community were supported by the video's stars. Social media profiles of the white shirt were shared with their tens of millions of global followers and Arsenal.com eloquently explained the power of the club shirt to bring about meaningful change:

'The shirt will become a symbol of positivity in the community, given to individuals and organisations who are giving back to the community and creating a positive environment for young people.'

Those awarded the shirts will immediately be shown as role models validated by the club that the overwhelming majority of the local community support. Where a trophy or certificate often has the unintended consequences of alienating and ridiculing the recipients from their peer groups an Arsenal shirt, especially one that cannot be bought, has tremendous currency and kudos that represents real achievement and a meaningful connection to the club that cannot be gazumped by those with money and access. They then become, like the ever-growing number of Her Game Too shirts that fundraise for the grassroots girls' game, beacons of hope in an otherwise desperate situation. Too many shirts have become calling cards for socially corrupting influences, but this initiative briefly wrests back the narrative to one of humanity and community. Never underestimate the power of a club shirt to do good when handled respectfully.

Of course, this being real life, not everything followed the script. Forest would win the game late on, leading some Forest fans to taunt the Gunners, 'Are you Tottenham in disguise?' But a bigger victory will be achieved if all this effort saves a single precious life.

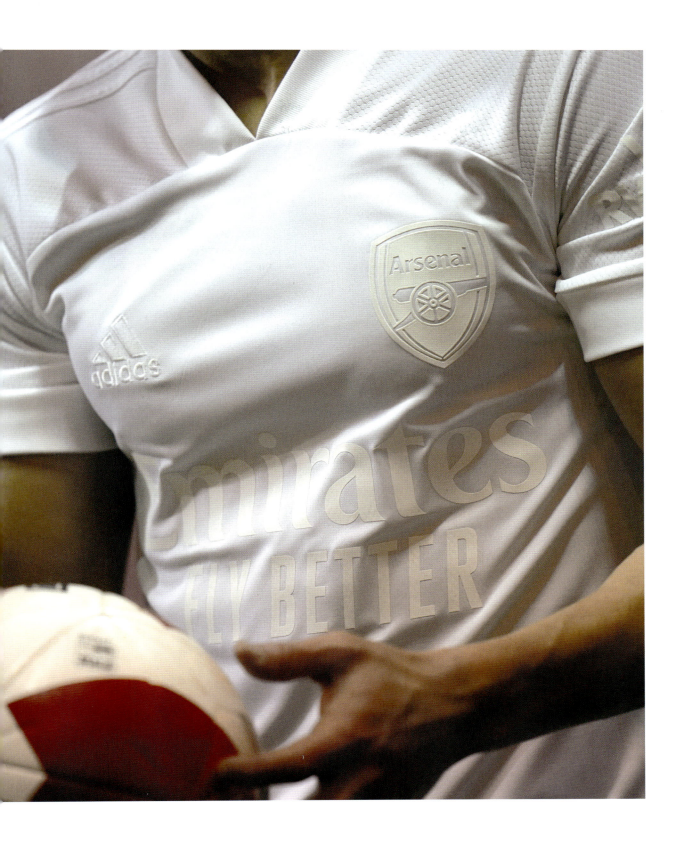

Mighty Fine Design

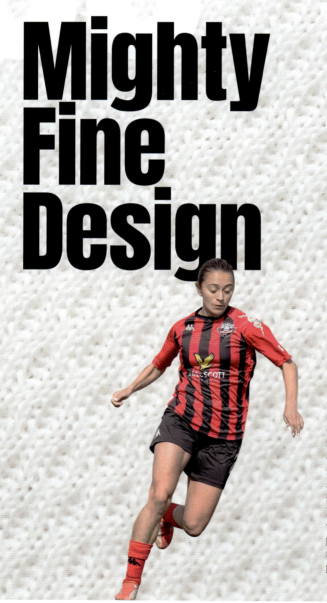

Good kit design is all about persuading the eye to go where you want it: usually the sponsor's logo and kit brand followed by the club crest in a distant third. The best real estate for any product is the top-left corner as our eyes, trained by a lifetime of reading from there, are primed to seek out anything shiny on the left rather than the right (unless you are a reader of Arabic or Urdu where words travel in the opposite direction).

Normally we as fans need to wait for our clubs to decide what we are going to buy, but some – amazingly without the help of NFTs – are giving fans options within a range of choices, or free rein. At Exeter City, members of the supporters' trust were given three options to vote on that riffed on the club's vertical stripes in early 2022. Impressively for a relatively small club, 1,010 trust members voted and 49 per cent agreed on the design, giving it strong momentum that will hopefully convert to healthy sales. For completely fan-owned club Lewes FC, their kit design for the 2022/23 women's and men's teams was a way to promote their app with all voting funnelled through it. In December 2021, owners (and I am proud to count myself as one) were given two final choices from the previously submitted designs and all the results were shared through their key platform. For a team in the Isthmian

League Premier Division, this was some highly impressive marketing.

With so much advanced technology, fans also have a chance to design their own kits. Concept kits have a strong online community sharing design and graphics tips as well as peer-reviewing each other's efforts. Twitter feeds like @ConceptKits often come up with designs showing far more passion and understanding of what a club stands for than imported agencies bent on maximising the return of investment. Some clubs have noticed this resource. Crewe Alexandra partnered @Konceptkitz (not to be confused with Concept Kits) in 2021 to design their third kit and for the 2022/23 season, they ran a campaign for another version.

On a much grander scale, Borussia Dortmund put together a design panel of high-profile players and designers including captain Marco Reus to review contributions from fans and designers alike for the 2023/24 season's home kit. This is a bold move to go for their iconic shirt rather than tuck the competition away in the third kit template. You have to warm to their admission that their previous efforts have not always worked:

'In 112 years of our club's history, we have already seen countless jerseys: from real classics to plain, gaudy, modern or wild jerseys to – yes, you have to admit that – some fashion escapades and total mistakes.'

This is an innovative way to connect with fans and designers and leverage their expertise to create a popular design. There is even far more opportunity for design when buying our pub team kits. Teamshirts.co.uk is one example of a company that lets you choose a base kit, upload your own design, select your font and text, names and numbers before letting them produce and finish the work. There are clearly limitations with no chance to design your crest, but it certainly makes your ragtag collection of hungover hoofers at least look smarter on a cold Sunday morning.

'And The Football Shirt Oscar Goes To'

Let's start with a stone-cold classic given a few new modern twists. The Ajax women's kit for the 2021/22 season is a homage to the Cruyff legend and the imperious team of the early 1970s. With its crew neck and slightly thinner red band than the modern version to fully evoke the glory days, it returns to the sponsorship from ABN Amro Banking like its original but adds enough small feature changes to stand out as more than a cut and paste. What really appeals to me is that, although the template for the men's and women's teams are the same, rather than having cable company Ziggo used by the men, the vertical classic of Amro for the women's team makes the kit so much more stylish. That both teams returned to the slightly outsized original crest for a single season just adds to the achingly nostalgic feel of the design, bringing back misty nights in Amsterdam watching dizzy defenders being tied in knots by the maestro Cruyff and his sinuous magic. And as for that crest – in its 2021 poll of the 100 greatest ever football badges, *FourFourTwo* gave the number one spot to 1860 Munich for its 'simple and classy' design. The runners-up spot went to Ajax and shows that it's not only the design of the logo that creates a resonance but what has happened at the club and how they are perceived. As Mark White et al purr:

'Considered one of the coolest clubs in Europe due to their Cruyffian philosophies and constant promotion of young talent, Ajax also have a pretty swish badge to match their beliefs. The gentleman featured on the crest of the Dutch giants is Ajax, a Greek hero and fabled warrior in Homer's Iliad. He is drawn using just 11 lines, the number of players on a football team. Ajax can't help but be cool, can they?'

They were to keep their coolness going in May 2021. To thank their fans for supporting them during the pandemic they melted down their Eredivisie trophy and converted it into tens of thousands of little silver stars as a gift for all of their season ticket holders.

Taking away the now common stars for championships won for the modern homage also declutters the chest and makes it feel more like a time machine than a tribute act. The design just oozes pure class, just like Cruyff et al.

An honourable mention goes to the cross design of Finland in Euro 2020, which takes the eyes on one of the most stylish journeys. Not only does the fading up of light blue from the base of the cross to navy on the right shoulder give our eyes nourishment, but the clean shape and use of only blue and white throughout the shirt (including the Nike logo and national crest) is clean

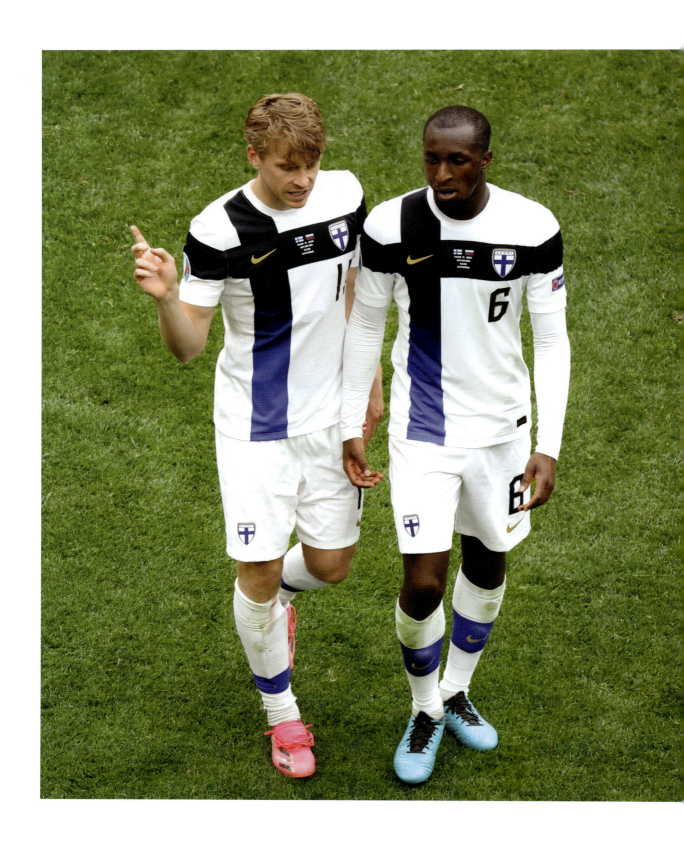

and calm. My only criticism is that the crosshairs of the design are placed on the right shoulder to arrive at the Nike swoosh rather than the left shoulder and heart (I know I'm old-fashioned, but the crest belongs over the heart).

For me, the best rendition of the cross design was created by Suphanburi FC, where I used to work. Named after the province just north of Bangkok, their 2015 kit hit all the high notes of shirt perfection. The cross not only framed and structured the design using metallic blue to contrast with the electric yellow, but by being split and tapered with a pause before the crest, the cross created a sense of energy and direction but also control that, literally, pointed to the club badge. The shirt also underscored a club narrative. As club president and Thai cabinet minister Varawut Silpa-archa (known affectionately as Top) told me, 'The cross represented the Arrows of Triumph for four groups of people. The arrow that runs from the bottom of the shirt up to the club's emblem represents support from fans both in Suphanburi, around the country and from abroad. The arrow running from the left arm to the club's emblem represents a commitment from players and staff. The one that runs from the right arm to the club's emblem represents continuous support from sponsors and partners both domestic and international to strengthen the image and position of the club in the Thai Premier League. The fourth and final arrow running from the top to the club's emblem represents

the continuous support, devotion and passion of the club's executive to see the club through its ups and downs while maintaining a smooth and effective running of the club. The four arrows mean all roads lead to the club and that every resource and effort shall be committed towards the triumphant future of Suphanburi Football Club.'

For my hat-trick of choices, I have to admit that, just like with the Falkland Islands home kit, I am a sucker for a sash – especially if it is in a cherry red and crosses the crest (and our heart, of course). But I also love to see a shirt design that tells a story. And if that narrative happens to combine with the St. Pauli I often lovingly refer to throughout the book, then I'm all in.

In January 2022 designers Kit and Bone unveiled a stunning creation for St. Pauli On Sea that I return to in chapter 17. There we review the way each shirt helps a local homeless charity in tandem with supporting the fight against homophobia. But for now, let's just luxuriate in this mightiest of fine designs. The narrow black collar starts the feeling of taut and focussed fashion where lines and designs are not distracted by floppy frippery. This black contrasts strongly with the base underlay white running through the top half of the front and most of the back. The skull extracted from the mother club's Jolly Roger centres the crest, sitting above their established (non-establishment) date of 2020, surrounded by the rainbow flag reimagined in wavy lines to reflect the club's close

Image: Matt Pascoe

connection to the sea. The green and yellow shoulder sash momentarily jars the eye before, like a freezing sorbet, it starts to offload its tart flavours.

The bottom half of the shirt resembles a sample of strident swatches held up for approval, with blocks of blue, black, green and yellow separating each polka dot section. Choosing several sections of polka dots infuses the shirt with a sense of humorous mischief, toying with something that is so out of fashion, it might just be fashionable, and if it isn't we confidently don't care. The way perspective is toyed with is also extremely appealing. Even the Kit and Bone logo reaches upwards and invites our eyes to rise towards the Norwich City palette left shoulder. Straight lines and curves nourish our eye lines and stop them from resting on anything static and staid.

And at the design's heart is the simple and compelling message, 'Love is Love'. After all the energy created around the logo, there is a calm centre for the message to breathe. Letters vary in width, again challenging the reading we expect with innovative and unusual visual journeys. This design makes a virtue of questioning some people's perceptions, just like the central message. But the designers also consider that very few of us, particularly like me in my middle age, look good in most skin-tight iterations. So the white section is for our upper torso, but the flurry of colours nicely shades our meaty girth and helps airbrush out the increasing curves. As Kit and Bone

diplomatically describe what the shirt chooses to highlight and camouflage:

'All of our football shirts are created with fans in mind. They are a regular cut, giving a great fit for all body types.'

In February 2022 I spoke to Kit and Bone's Matt Pascoe to find out more about the shirt's story. He told me:

'We started by taking the waves from their badge and extending that pattern to fill our page. Then we recoloured the lines to bring in the #pride flag at the heart of this design. But we knew this didn't go anywhere near far enough in terms of pushing the design's limits. So we then set about cutting up the pattern into big slices and rescaling them to create something far bolder and more interesting than where we'd started. The result is an abstract wave of pop colours and energy, designed to be truly visible.'

This is such a nourishing and challenging design that it bears regular viewing and tells a story that doesn't grow old. There is also a similar tone to the FSV Mainz 05 'carnival kit' that we look at in chapter 16. Strident colours that confront and play with perspective (and also help support local charities). I have to admit that I don't know if, as a 54-year-old, I can carry off the Kit and Bone creation, but it certainly makes me want to put that cheeseburger down and head to the gym for one last try.

In May 2021 music, fashion and culture magazine *The Face* interviewed Martine Rose about her process of designing a new England shirt. She clearly wasn't the first designer to collaborate with football. In 2006, PSG wore a Louis Vuitton-style away shirt and in 2014 Real Madrid collaborated with Japanese designer Yohji Yamamoto to create a stylish, Asian art-inflected third shirt, but Rose was invested in this project in a way rarely seen before. Described by journalist Matthew Whitehouse as someone who had previously built a career that 'cultivated a world around communities, tribes and subcultures' made her an ideal candidate to enter the world of football kit designs.

Her collaboration with Nike to produce 'The Lost Lionesses' shirt draws on the heroism of the 1971 women's team to produce a genderless creation described as 'a subversive take on a recognised icon'. That year will always go down as the moment women's football completed its shameful half-century ban. This England team played in front of 90,000 fans at the Azteca Stadium in Mexico City and, although they were knocked out of the Women's World Cup in the group stage, they were treated amazingly by the locals. Not so by their own federation. On their return home, they were banned for three months by the WFA, which was in the process of establishing an official England team.

The subversion comes with the England badge being counterpoised by a Martine Rose crest in a fully reversible style. In conversation with the journalist, Rose hit on one of the key motivators to reinvent our club shirts in a respectful but innovative way:

'Some of the stories that we want to tell—how can we tell them through a shirt? It's one of the reasons why I like menswear: there are rules. That's the thing when you're working with something as iconic, well-known, huge and epic as an England shirt: it's the rules. It's fun to push against those rules. It's fun to see how far you can take it until it doesn't become an England shirt anymore. I mean, as a person I don't like rules. But I like rules to work in.'

To be seen as part of a club's culture, shirts need to have a sense of resonance and narrative. Design decisions need to be made through a thorough understanding of what the club represents or aspires to represent. Otherwise, shirts are no more than white noise: full of sound and fury but signifying nothing.

Into this disruptive and innovative kit design environment come Castore. Based in Manchester after being founded in Liverpool, Castore has had a meteoric rise for a company only started in 2015 and already selling its goods in 50 countries. Founders Tom and Phil Beahon shared with their website in September 2021 how the capture of Glasgow Rangers was a key driver for their subsequent growth. Rather like Her Game Too partnering Everton in December of the same year, getting a marquee signing not only energises your staff and the partners you already have, but opens the door to a new stage in scalability, profile and enhanced turnover. Their momentum was also enhanced because, wearing Castore shirts for the first time, Rangers went the whole season undefeated, creating a powerful narrative to share with other potential recruits.

That Rangers were Castore's first partner – who, like Leeds' title-winning season when they signed with Admiral – was a vindication of the brand and all that it stands for (even the eye-watering price of some goods). Consumers are much more likely to part with £105 for a pair of plain jogging pants or £695 for a ski jacket if the brand is tangibly connected to success. Although the Scottish Premier League is considered by UEFA's club coefficient rankings as Europe's ninth most successful league behind Austria, Rangers have a huge global and committed fanbase that Castore can tap into. This was remarkably savvy by the brothers as,

while so many brands were stampeding towards the Premier League titans, they saw the opportunity to get huge resonance at a relatively low price point. There is also another similarity to the Admiral and Leeds deal through Don Revie. Steven Gerrard's stellar season at Rangers led to him being snapped up by Aston Villa, whose new kit for the 2022/23 season was by Castore.

The Beahon boys also showed nimble innovation by wrapping their business around an overarching ethos of 'Better Never Stops' to help differentiate their products and company culture in a hugely competitive marketplace.

Their huge ambition also shows a determination to expand exponentially. Admiral rather naively stumbled from making nuns' knickers to international football kits without a strategy. Castore know what they want to achieve, how they aim to do it and who they want to do it with.

The company stated, 'From day one, our ambition for Castore has always been to build a global brand, one that competed on the world stage with the titans who dominated the sportswear market when we were growing up. Despite the many challenges, hardships and setbacks we have faced in the last five years, July 2021 will forever be a seminal moment for us as it marked the moment Castore entered the English Premier League through our partnerships with Wolverhampton Wanderers and Newcastle United.'

There is also something disarmingly quaint about the brothers' approach to business. Rather than the alpha male posturing of the cabal of billionaires, they understand that, if they pause, they could be swallowed up, so relentless energy, innovation and growth are their only options in a marketplace notorious for fickle and destructive decisions, as Admiral found to their cost.

'It's not intellect or strategy that has got us this far, but a single-minded commitment to being disruptive and finding ways of doing old things differently, whilst trusting creativity and never giving up no matter how crazy some people think (and have told us) we are.'

Clearly fewer and fewer people are questioning their sanity. By February 2022, Bundesliga high-flyers Bayer Leverkusen had signed a five-year contract for the men's and women's team as well as launching a black and red Castore leisure range.

To see just how disruptive Castore has been, we only need to review Admiral's website in 2022. They are trying to reinvent themselves as a savvy and cutting-edge brand. But, for every innovation, the list of clubs from the Professional Development League and US Youth Soccer League drags down any momentum they are trying to build. When your international partners are Turks and Caicos Islands – ranked 204 with FIFA – and few of your clubs have any resonance with consumers, you can have as many 3D kit design applications as you want. It is also telling that their website history ribbon is dominated by football until 1991 when Leeds United won the First Division title wearing their brand, but from then it switches to cricket and a fashion brand launched in 2011. They tried to return the focus to football in 2015 with their capture of AFC Wimbledon but returned to a push of 'casual fashion' the following year knowing that their football ship had sailed and they were now near the bottom of the manufacturing food chain.

People look elsewhere not only for the established brands dominating the game but new and upcoming market disruptors. Castore's rapid growth in some ways describes Admiral's early days but, for their sake, we have to hope their story will be more sustainable.

04

Atalanta.
From the Cradle to the Shave

With a population of only 120,000 the city of Bergamo knows that, to stop young fans migrating to the glamorous Milan clubs on its doorstep, it has to catch them young. So, in 2018, rather than spend the money they gained from their fourth-placed Serie A finish the season before on a flashy, ephemeral new player, they decided to invest in the world's youngest youth team. Highly respected club president Antonio Percassi green-lit the project to give every baby born in the area a box containing locally produced milk and a newborn-sized home shirt.

The baby doesn't even need to be born in the region. The club offers the gift box to any global mother. How the recovering new mums feel about this was not documented, but as a piece of marketing it is genius. Already in a tight-knit community with default local support, they are feeding a flame already burning fiercely. Taking the sponsors' logos off was also a shrewd move to stop criticisms of mere brand profile expansion for the companies that underwrite the club. This is particularly important as Plus 500 specialise in CFDs (Contracts for Differences) – a turbocharged way to lose your life savings in an 'investment' many customers don't understand until it is too late are their main shirt sponsors.

You have to wonder what local arch-rivals Brescia make of this post-natal cultural imperialism. Fighting for promotion from Serie B, they know that Atalanta's baby boom has stolen a march on them and futureproofed their fanbase before potential supporters think about which club to follow whose stadiums are only 60km apart. Talking to Copa 90's Eli Mengem in January

2020, Atalanta's foetal correspondent Matteo proudly showed the Jenga of boxes targeting all the hospitals in the region and helped give out the personal letters from the club president to the recovering mother. For those who have just delivered an appropriately named Black and Blue (and it's heartening to see the club targets 'babies', not 'boys') you can picture the recovering mum rolling her eyes as football invades her life even earlier than she had anticipated.

What gives this idea heft is that, unlike the burgeoning pop-up agreements with shady betting sites routed through Malta (taking advantage of their 0.5 per cent tax rate) this is a club playing the long game. The results may take a decade to come through, but it puts the club's name at the core of kindergarten conversations and is pushing against an open door with a wider community already passionately intoxicated by 'The Goddess'. It's also a long-term strategy rather than a short-term financial shock tactic showing that, like the much-loved president's decade-long and counting ownership of the club, planting seeds trumps buying the forest.

With a stadium that only holds 21,300 there isn't much spare capacity to welcome this nappied legion but, making this symbiosis between club and community central to both, moves the relationship on from distant adoration to making meaningful change together. The giddy early stages of a relationship strewn with gesturing moves to a deep bond where each partner instinctively knows what the other is thinking and senses their needs in *sympatico*.

Plunged into chaos and plagued by sirens at the epicentre of the European outbreak of Covid in the spring of 2020, Bergamo also came together by constructing a field hospital in only ten days at a local exhibition centre. It would open on 8 April to protect the main Ospedale Papa Giovanni XIII hospital from total collapse. All hands went up and many came from the ultras in Atalanta's fiercely loyal Curva Nord. Talking to *The Guardian*'s Nick Ames, Dr Oliviero Valoti recalled:

'You'd see these people wearing an Atalanta jersey, running around from left to right, transporting materials and setting up panels to divide different departments … People with tears in their eyes as they worked, trying to take the smallest amount of time possible but while still doing everything perfectly, not just quickly.'

One of the most poignant examples of the power a shirt can hold came when Jürgen Griesback stunned by the murder of Colombian defender Andrés Escobar following his own goal in the 1994 World Cup, set up Football For Peace (*Fútbol por la Paz*) in honour of the fallen player using football among the drug war-torn streets of Medellín to find a measure of normality.

He explained, 'At its peak, *Fútbol por la Paz* had more than 10,000 regular players from across every district of Medellín, and the number two shirt worn by all participants – in recognition of the jersey worn by Andrés – became accepted currency for travel across the city's bus network. As such, the shirts not only meant that players could afford to travel to matches, they also acted as a passport, enabling them to travel unharmed through rival territories, such was the respect with which *Fútbol por la Paz* came to be universally regarded. The jersey became something that young people were proud to be seen wearing, as a symbol of their courage and solidarity in the pursuit of peace.'[3]

At Atalanta, Ames goes on to describe how the players have embedded themselves into this culture of collegiality 'even though they are stars now and only two of the squad were born locally. They come from 14 countries but none of them left Bergamo during lockdown; the trauma was more than distant bad news.'[4]

Another beautiful example of collegiality happened on 3 March 2022. Despite dealing with the fallout of having three major Russian sponsors and an owner ejected from their club accompanied with their oceans of money, Everton found out that both of their FA Cup fifth-round opponents' kits would clash with their own. So they

[3] Fleming, S., *Radical Football: Jürgen Griesbeck and the Story of Football for Good*, p58 (Pitch Publishing, Kindle edition)

[4] *The Guardian*, 11 August 2020: www.theguardian.com/football/2020/aug/11/atalanta-results-are-a-really-important-cure-covid19-bergamo-people-champions-league

paid for a bespoke Puma kit (I can hear the shirt collectors salivating as I type this). Boreham Wood's all-white home number would have clashed with Everton's socks and shorts, while their blue away kit also wouldn't work.

The solution was not only elegant but rooted in history. For football in general, from the 1880s until 1992, no teams were allowed to have black kits. That colour was reserved for the officials who could wear tailored jackets or blazers in the early years (something that desperately needs reviving) until the first Premier League season where they started with green and have criss-crossed the colour palettes ever since. To this day, in a rather quaint and 'other' approach, black kits remain banned in National League competitions. Their officials still toe the black line, probably because they don't get paid enough to trot out in an odyssey in 'medium fawn' or chartreuse. Everton's design for Boreham Wood was black with flashes of green and yellow finished with embroidery on the chest to mark the occasion. The Toffees even pitched in to help the club travel up from Hertfordshire the night before and contributed to their accommodation expenses. A beautiful gesture, although the cynic might say Everton could just as easily have changed their shorts and socks.

Atalanta may have a much smaller budget than their Serie A rivals, but they have a club culture and fierce loyalty allied to the deep respect of their owner that keeps them punching way above their weight. Few clubs other than they or Leicester City can grow in the safe hands of sound stewardship and an opportunistic eye on the future.

Would this diaper diplomacy work in England? London hospitals would probably struggle to satisfy the demand for Manchester United romper suits, but, for provincial clubs whose main USP is their close-knit fanbase, it could have a chance to take hold. Of course, with grasping billionaires ruling the laughingly called 'football pyramid' who espouse the lie that is trickle-down economics while trousering every penny they can, hopes are slim. Even when, as with Manchester United, results are poor, owners like the Glazers awarded themselves an £11m dividend on 7 January 2022, which must feel like another gut punch to the United faithful. Michael Calvin in *Whose Game is it Anyway?* agrees that the 'pyramid' is a smokescreen perpetuated by those at the top like Manchester City CEO Ferran Soriano who, 'Clearly had no conception of the culture he was threatening. In his eyes, the pyramid was nothing more than a talent pipeline ready to be adapted to serve his purposes.'[5]

Lower league clubs simply don't have the funds for such a grand gesture and our football fan dynasties seem more fractured than the Bergamo duopoly. My local city Exeter would have maternity wards with allegiances split between The Grecians, Plymouth, Torquay, Yeovil and the usual procession of national and international brands.

[5] Calvin, M., *Whose Game Is It Anyway?: Football, Life, Love & Loss*, p258-259 (Pitch Publishing, Kindle edition)

05
Cash for Trash

Line Up For Your Super League Shirts

Avoiding the digital piles of work awaiting my urgent attention allows me to dream of my next trip to Villa Park. In the work-avoidance fantasy, we welcome Chelsea to our Theatre of Mediocrity.

They pile through the Aston streets and as they are funnelled between rows of fluorescent police the home fans are held back from the usual 'if it wasn't for that police horse, I'd 'ave ya' bravado. But this time, something is different. As well as the usual anti-Russian/oligarch/Cockerny invective, there is a building chant from my daydream belief. 'When the fans are united, they can never be divided' is undercut with overhead clapping aimed at the Chelsea contingent. As they look up at the stand they are entering, a huge banner is unfurled by two of the home fans to greet them. 'Speak Truth to Power. Villa fans Salute Chelsea's Supporters.' Clearly, in reality, there would be no apostrophe and rather than a pseudo-political statement it would have been a minefield of F and C bombs but hey: it's my daydream so give me some latitude.

As the toxic dust settled from the hangover-length European Franchise League, acres of print and litres of oxygen have been expelled about the ferociously odious Florentino Pérez and the conniving JP Morgan spotting a chance to leverage even more debt into football in return for a fingerhold in a new market rich for exploitation. They also cunningly recoiled from the line of post-covidiot fire and used the gormless, preening peacocks in Madrid and Barcelona as human shields. But what few have yet to focus on in this febrile arena of anger is the mutual respect brewing between fans and how dangerous that is for the debt-drunk footballing cartels that create an environment where 'legacy fans' are treated like leeches. By disenfranchising them from the clubs they have supported for generations, transient owners are pushing them towards new and iconoclastic collegiality.

Clubs need us to hate our opposition. It helps drive merchandise sales that have already been banked by clubs through prepaid agreements but, through our revenge spending, they can drive up the next front-loaded cash drop by global kit manufacturers. If we start to disconnect the opposing owners from the fans, loathe one and respect the other then the whole hate speech construction starts to totter. If fans talk to each other and share stories then we can see they are like us. Matchdays will still contain anger and frustration from weekend warriors taking two days away from their deadening job, but that hate will not be wasted on the group heading towards us whose only difference is their heartfelt allegiance to a different crest over history. Instead, it will be universally focussed on the dead-eyed suits viewing

their fiefdom below, gathering up social media moments to use for future price rises and share price hikes from signing superstars past their sell-by date. They need us to fool ourselves into financing their latest golden dividend payment or consultancy fee for a job they already have in a club they already own.

Remarkably, the Franchise League website is still live, sharing its bullish philosophy of, astonishingly, solidarity and sustainability. This is a message parallel to a Number 10 drinks non-party and someone would have been strongly advised to take the site down to avoid further ridicule. Its account on the petri dish of conflict, Twitter, has been suspended, but the website stands as an image of hubris as glamorous as a row of broken teeth.

Shared moments are the common denominator in every game. They come from each step we take towards the stadium and can't be monetised or spun for funds. It is the look you get from the train ticket inspector spotting your football shirt who hates his job and wishes he was joining you at the game. It's the routines and strange obsessions (looking at you, Kevin Day, and your special route to Selhurst Park) we often share that we know are pointless but give us hope that we have helped the team in some odd way. The childish freedoms of dressing up in cheap plastic clothes expensively bought. Goals and action are certainly not our main aim. Shared moments are both a platform and catalyst for everything else that happens in the game and were one of the reasons for the failure of the Franchise League. The Dirty Dozen teams, led by Real's own Arthur Slugworth Florentino Pérez, wanted to get the Golden Ticket that gave access to Willy Wonka's football factory. But they forgot that they are, like Mr Wonka, simply custodians whose fleeting time will soon pass while the game lives on with them as a fading memory. Wonka realised that the only person to carry his legacy forward was Charlie Bucket when Pérez went all in on Mike TeaVee. Here's to all the Charlies and long live the legacy fans.

'Happy Monday, everyone. Hope you all had a great weekend. Now I've been a busy bee. As you know, a cool new European Super League is starting in a few months, and I thought we should be ahead of the curve. So, I sourced 70,000 shirts to celebrate this amazing new era. We might be a High Street sports store, but I've been thinking outside the box and I see this as a tentpole product to really activate a new customer demographic. I've set the price at £29.99 so we can cream the profit in. They only cost £3 from our Vietnamese sweatshop. So. Any questions? Can you all stop shouting? No: I haven't lost my fricking mind.'

Fans nostalgic for the 48-hour era that was the European Franchise League can now mark its disorderly retreat that made *Dad's Army* seem like the SAS through investment in a range of polyester monstrosities. Ironically, given the £3bn fronted by the weasely bankers at JP Morgan, you only need to source a couple of pounds to get hold of one of history's strangest souvenirs via the graveyard of bad ideas at wholesaleclearance.co.uk. Originally aimed to be flogged at £30, this 93 per cent discount still seems a few per cent above its intrinsic value.

Without a hint of irony, the shirts proudly display 'new era' across the chest. Better slogans would have been 'Shorter Than a Bad Hangover' or 'Bielsa's Lazio Era'.

The store that messed up so badly hasn't even had the courage to be named. Instead, journalists risking lawyers' letters must tiptoe around the 'High Street Sports Chain' hint. It would have been an ideal chance for the company to revel in their stupidity and enter the long line of 'all publicity is good publicity' campaigns like Greggs's vegan sausage rolls that used the imbecilic outrage of Piers Morgan to drive their campaign. As they sprung their trap for the former presenter, their Twitter feed went into full Bond villain mode:

'We've been expecting you, Mr Morgan.'

'Don't worry if passersby are laughing behind your back.'

The High Street chain store could learn a lesson from Wholesale Clearance who go full *mea culpa* in their 'promotion' of their latest bankrupt of ideas stock, 'A "new era" as the shirts say but now the Super League has been sidelined, these are now limited-edition time capsules of the worst 48 hours for any football fan. So, if you want to be a proud owner of one of these shirts to remind yourselves of how terrible the owners still are, now is your chance. These would also make a good present for your friends who support a top-six side or, if you simply want to buy it to burn it and tear it up on arrival, our offer can help with that too.'

Their customers seem to agree when posting comments below the page. Aden Jones shares how he 'would love one of these to go on my scarecrows on the farm', and Marilyn Blake 'would like a red one please to wipe the dog's paws after a muddy walk'. Florentino Pérez must be spinning in his gold-plated jacuzzi.

The other five teams have their names on them, including City, but for 'Manchester' they might have been waiting for an additional 'Wildcats' or 'Outrage' to complete the brand personality. These shirts have become tombstones to mark the passing of any semblance of sanity by dumb billionaires who will only regroup and go again once the coast is clear.

Cud's 1992 indie classic 'Rich and Strange' feels like the soundtrack to Wholesale Clearance's grand launch.

The lights dim and, floating through a sea of dry ice, we see the CEOs from the Greedy Six carried aloft by players and staff from the Other Fourteen as Cud's anthem blasts out:

'I'm never fed up,
Because I'm made up,
Head full of loose change,
Because I'm rich and strange.

Holy Moses, here we go again,
Headlong into some crazy scheme,
Success no more a pipe dream.'

Cheekily, on 23 November 2021, the Harrods of the bargain bin relaunched the range 'from £19.99' (they were all that price) with a highly hopeful promotional copy (and an increase of £17.99 a shirt).

'Looking for the perfect secret Santa gift for a football fan? Remember the diabolical European Super League earlier this year? Imagine the look on your football friend's face when they open their prezzie to find their Club's Super League Shirt. As featured in the *Sun*, *Mail*, *Mirror*, Fox News and more. Shirts have been selling exceptionally well, so don't miss out on your chance to either own a piece of humorous history or wind up your mate this Christmas!'

This had the kind of gormless optimism shown by the European robber barons. It must be contagious.

06

As Seen on Screen

The reluctant star of the BBC comedy/mockumentary *This Country*, Kerry Mucklowe is permanently squeezed into the shirt of her begrudgingly beloved Swindon Town. Kerry's (lack of) clothes choices show how football kits, pre-empting lockdown and its two sequels as unwelcome as Little Fockers, help us divide our lives into three manageable states:

Wear it. Wash it. Dry it.

This Zen approach to clothes choices frees Kerry's mind, like Steve Jobs and Mark Zuckerberg before her. Famous for choosing the narrowest range of clothes, Kerry's soulmates knew they could free mental 'bandwidth' by uncluttering the everyday choices to zero in on the biggest of issues unencumbered by daily and seasonal fashion compromises. This also leaves Kerry free to contemplate deeper concepts like financial independence:

'Me and Kurtan are gonna have a flat in the middle of the village, and all our furniture will be inflatable, and we'll have a Sky box, and it's all gonna pay for itself because we'll use the spare bedroom to breed quails because their eggs are worth f***ing s***loads.'

Or social justice:

'There's a balance between being nice and being feared. Like Dr Barnado. He was just too nice and not feared, so he just got overrun by orphans and everyone just took the piss.'

The 2020/21 'Season of the Sofa' forced us all to live the Mucklowe life and football kits helped us do it. Kerry's clothes decisions are binary. Warm and it's the shirt; cold and it's the shirt and a coat. Football shirts give her an inelegant solution to our newly (and her permanently) sedentary world through these reassuringly simple sartorial solutions. They also made us feel that we were keeping fit. Footballers are fit and strong. We wear their shirts, so we are healthy by proxy. There was no need for Joe Wicks. We had it (and us) covered from the sofa.

Kerry is a taliswoman for kits as comforters, as barricades against an uncertain world. The shirt roots her in her Wiltshire homeland and signals how she has no time for pointless activities like work or study. Not for her the heady escapism of PSG or Barcelona shirts. She loathes and needs her deadbeat community: her shirt and Swindon's history are her antidotes to aspiration. She sides with John Cleese's character Brian Stimpson in *Clockwise*:

'It's not the despair, Laura. I can take the despair. It's the hope I can't stand.'

When your club's honours board lists ten titles in the Wiltshire County Senior Cup, two Southern League titles and one Western League, then Kerry knows that the low/no bar set by Swindon's shirt perfectly matches her own. The top becomes a touchstone for her passive-aggressive nihilism and bluntly declares, 'Don't confuse me with someone who cares.' If the Malaysian saying 'everyone hears the tree fall but nobody hears the forest growing' is meant to inspire our Kerry, she will be straight round to Kurtan's house asking for a chainsaw.

In a surreal twist, Swindon Town unveiled a statue to Kerry that is based on Rodin's *The Thinker*. The beautiful irony is that living in the Robins' kit allows her to wallow in the opposite. There is no need to think about trips to Old Trafford or the Emirates a decade and a half into bouncing between the third and fourth tier. There is something innately freeing that consistent failure brings. Real success is an imposter not to be trusted. Promotion to League One was just enough excitement to process, but not enough to destabilise this existence, forged with a familiarity that breeds comforting contempt. Luckily, the following season's immediate relegation back to the fourth tier stopped Kerry from getting too glass half full. An oil-rich Gulf Arab tycoon catapulting the club to Premier League glory would be greeted by distrustful antagonism from her because it would invite comparisons to her own life's story arc; searching for any kind of low-level attention as long as it doesn't involve work.

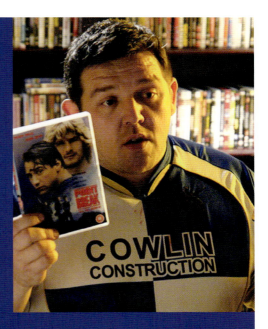

'I've got enemies in South Cerney, I've got enemies in North Cerney, I've got enemies in Cerney Wick. I've got enemies in Bourton-on-the-Water. There's a tea room there and under the counter, they've got a panic button and if I take one step inside, they can press that.'

She can seek out the points of least resistance in her forgotten rural town existence. Without the shirt, she would be just another nondescript Sports Direct fashionista. With it, her shirt of hurt singles her out as the person who looks like she cares for a club but doesn't, chooses to support her local team but does nothing else to show it and, when I trawled through the *This Country* scripts, never even explicitly names the team shirt she spends her life slouched inside.

Another film using the shirt of a perennially underachieving club draped over someone equally unmotivated came in 2007's *Hot Fuzz*. Like *This Country*, it was also based in the gateway to the south-west (always a fertile location for underachieving clubs). *Fuzz* was based in Somerset and saw a perfect local village beset by a strangely high number of 'aaaccidents'. PC Danny Butterman only entered the police force because his loving dad (and, spoiler alert, serial murderer) wanted him to. His job's only purpose was to pay for his lagers at the Sandford pub. What better club shirt to be wearing

than basement dwellers Bristol Rovers?

In his first scene propping up the bar, we can see all we need to know about him. Like the Pirates, this Gashead's horizons go no further than this parochial parish where nothing ever seems to happen (apart from a death toll that rivals a war zone). Like Kerry, he could have worn a Barcelona (or even Plymouth Argyle) shirt to show his upward mobility. But Rovers, as they tumble down the divisions, stop Danny from dreaming there is anything else to aspire to other than Cornettos and cake. There was clearly more than a nod to Rovers from the scriptwriter. Their fans sing a song called 'Goodnight, Irene' – Danny's beloved deceased mum was called Irene.

A strange football shirt and drama crossover had happened four years earlier when Chievo were sponsored by *Bad Boys II*. *Non hai'visto cattivi ragazzi due*? Bizarre, but not as odd as Altay İzmir in Turkey's top division who wore the name of Page 3 girl turned 'actor' and 'singer' Samantha Fox on their shirts in 1988 as a one-off before she played a concert in İzmir later that month. I'll just leave that with you.

KIT&CABOODLE

Mean Machine

Would you swap shirts with this man? Matthew Vaughn's 2001 promedy (as no one is calling it) prison comedy could only have a shirt as black as a Spinal Tap album cover. Appearing as Danny 'the Mean Machine' Meehan, Vinnie Jones could never have played his brutalist and unforgiving style of football (some roles just don't need acting) in a cerise or lilac anthem jacket. The shirt logo had to be the skull and crossbones used on St. Pauli and Forest Green Rovers shirts, but this skull was for headbutting not saving the planet and the crossbones would have been smashed over a prison guard's head in a riot. *Esquire* ranked the goal Meehan scored as number seven in the best last-minute goals in the movies (no prizes for guessing *Escape to Victory* came in first). Meehan deftly flicks the ball over a statuesque defender and rounds the keeper before laying it off to Danny ('Billy the Limpet') Dyer to score, which is where Jones really had to act after a career impersonating a head-on car crash. Meehan had been told to throw the game or risk another two decades in the slammer, but he was having none of it. As hard as coffin nails.

For those of us of a certain age, 1984's mockumentary *This Is Spinal Tap* saw a man mired in mediocrity choosing the club that fitted him like a leatherette glove. The bassist for the eponymous pompous and ageing rockers, Derek Smalls' father was based in the Midlands where he ran his telephone sanitisation empire. Seizing his opportunity in 1967 with the departure of Ronnie Pudding, Smalls describes David St Hubbins and Nigel Tufnel as 'like fire and ice' while his role was 'in the middle of that, kind of like lukewarm water'. Despite the sacrilege of wearing a West Ham baseball cap in some scenes, it is his allegiance to Shrewsbury Town that was immortalised in an airport security scene involving tin foil, a courgette and an extremely disturbed security guard. I grew up on the terraces at Shrewsbury where the fans would chant, 'We're not going up, we're not going down, we are Shrewsbury, we are Shrewsbury, we are Shrewsbury Town.'

For Smalls, the passive and pipe-smoking pseud, Shrewsbury were the ideal choice of club. Their minor achievements are mostly in the past (Town can boast being Third Division champions in 1979 and Smalls was the face of Belgian snack Floop). Easy to see but hard to notice, Smalls and Shrewsbury were a match made in Rock n Roll Heaven.

'Marty DiBergi: I remember being knocked out by their… their exuberance, their raw power… and their punctuality.'

Hooray for Hollyrood

A surprising Hollywood/Hollyrood crossover happened at the end of 2021 when HBO's *Succession*, after mentioning Edinburgh's Heart of Midlothian in a previous series, went one better and conducted a fictional takeover in its third season. The storyline saw Roman Roy buying the club to impress his father Logan, who he thinks is a Hearts follower. The cunning plot twist comes when he later discovers that his dad is in fact a fan of their intercity rivals Hibs. Ouch. To promote the storyline, 95 *Succession* shirts were produced for the club. Fans had to search through their social media platforms to find out how to grab one: an effective way to activate a fanbase in a club that has a fraction of the media momentum enjoyed by the two Glasgow giants. With the fictional company Waystar Royco on the front and *Succession* on the back, the launch was conducted via NOW TV and merged the shirts with fiction, the club with the series and the NOW TV on-demand viewing platform with subscription-fuelled HBO. Purchasing,

viewing, fiction and reality are being folded in further and further with every new marketing campaign.

Jumping further down the reality-bending small screen, fans of AFC Richmond, the fictional team run by Ted Lasso, can now buy merchandise for their favourite non-existent team through the Warner Bros online store. The football equivalent of wearing a Spinal Tap shirt, for a mere £51 you can pretend to be a fan by wearing the same shirt worn by actors pretending to be players for the club that pretends to play football in England. Surreal. Is your head-spinning yet? On 7 March 2022, as Richmond prepared for their third season in the Premier League, (sandwiching a small blip of relegation in season two) their fictional shirt sponsor Verani Sports was replaced by Nike. One of the last fictional shirt partners remains though. The Bantr dating app is front and centre which, considering a gambling or Socios brand would happily pay for that real estate, keeps some semblance of fictional purity in a discombobulating Ted Lasso world.

'If that's a joke, I love it. If not, can't wait to unpack that with you later.'

07

Looking back on the legendary player (and later manager) Roy Race's shirts over the second half of the 20th century tells us plenty about the club's evolution and the values *Roy of the Rovers* tried to uphold.

Melchester Rovers

Everyone's Favourite Second Club

Unfortunately, the story arcs were diverging more and more from society's headlong rush to rampant consumerism. A key story tactic was what film critic Mark Kermode calls 'Basil Exposition'. Members of the crowd who would set up the goalscoring punchline with a 'Racey's had a shot!' or 'the keeper won't make it!' had moved from being quaint to old-fashioned and out of step with the times. Loyal readers may have suspended disbelief, but the exploits of Billy the Fish for *Viz*'s Fulchester United were increasingly seen as more relevant as arch irony replaced innocent escapism. Sadly Roy, despite surviving five kidnappings in a decade, was also to lose his legendary left foot in a 1993 helicopter crash. Even a comic book character can't come back from that kind of setback.

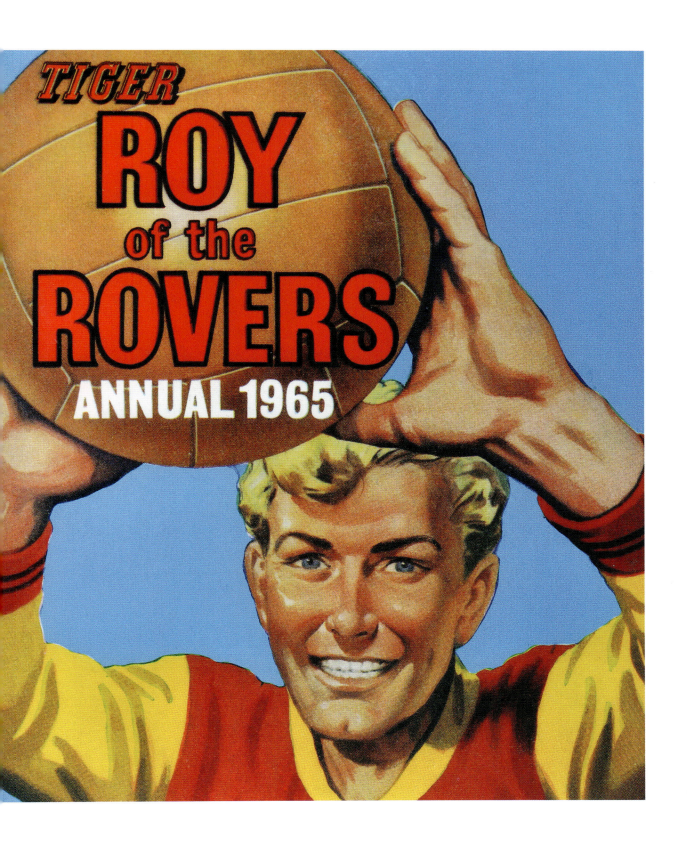

As John Devlin wrote in his excellent homage to the club[6], Melchester first played in the kind of utilitarian kit that would have gained a couple of rain-soaked kilos during a match. Roy was to make his debut in this. For the mid-1950s, going with a wing collar was the apex of futuristic design when clubs in the real world would be just as likely to go with no collars or simple string. A club with a similar colour palette to Melchester, Partick Thistle, showed how the real world would sometimes mirror or move away from the Melchester kit designers. Their 1950s kits had horizontal hoops of red and yellow with a wing collar for the long-sleeved shirt and a v-neck for the short-sleeved version. The design would be revisited in 2010, if not the collars. Maybe the designers thought an extra bit of collar would help keep out the biting wind of a bitter Glasgow winter.

By the mid-1960s, Melchester's designers had decided to add the club badge to the shirt. Again, this was an innovative decision given that most

[6] Devlin, J., *Melchester Rovers Kits 1956–2001*, retrieved 17 August 2021 from www.truecoloursfootballkits.com/2009/04/23/melchester-rovers-kits-1956-1973/

real-world clubs were yet to do the same. With its round-neck collar, it was worn until the early 1970s, although the badge was mysteriously to last only for one year. Probably the cartoonists didn't fancy having to add the level of detailing needed as the next comic deadline rapidly approached. The Jags would also adopt a rounded collar through the 1960s and left the kit design pretty much alone as they trudged through Scotland's footballing lower reaches.

In 1973, what many readers consider the iconic Melchester Rovers kit was created. Inverted for the away number, the home design was made up of red with a vertical yellow line that continues on the opposite side of the shorts. Even the socks were funkily futuristic, sporting a yellow 'T' design. It's a surprise that real-world clubs have not followed their fashion lead. Numbers on the sleeves was a classy touch and nod to the innovative numbering on Leeds United kits that season with their 'smiley-faced crest'. This bold and confident kit statement was worn until disaster struck in 1981

and the team were relegated. Suitably chastised, Melchester reverted to a more conservative symmetrical design. For Partick, they would also embrace the lurid colour codes of the 1970s by changing their home kit to a Liverpool 2021 third kit-style homage to Ronald McDonald with the yellow amp turned up to 11 and a red collar completing the Big Mac vibe; something that Melchester would, unfortunately, replicate at the turn of the new decade.

Partick were to change direction in the mid-1970s (you have to assume by public demand) and go back to stripes. This time they would be vertical rather than horizontal and would be a staple of most kits moving forward. The Jags would also start to use their shirts for sponsors, starting in the early '80s with West Glasgow's favourite bakery Mortons Rolls. The '80s and '90s would also see them sponsored by local curry house Ashoka West End, local soft furnishing experts Texstyle World and 'the home of innovative engineering solutions' Watson Towers. Oh. the glamour.

Melchester were also to reflect how Liverpool's Hitachi deal in 1979 was about to open the floodgates to shirts as billboards when in 1981, a decade before football's Big Bang, they added their first shirt sponsor. Gola was not only on front and centre but part of one of Melchester's most elegant designs that combined with a newly created club crest. Unfortunately, the Gola deal was only to last a year and, while real-world clubs were being showered with commercial revenue, *Roy of the Rovers* was beginning to start its existential decline. Unlike the increasing carousel of kits in real-world teams, Melchester would rarely appear in away kits. In the 1980s they would rotate between a plain blue shirt, a yellow one or an all-white design. White became increasingly popular after 1992 and I can't help thinking that this was to cut down on the cartoonists' billable hours as budget after budget was being slashed to extinction. There was a glimmer of hope half a decade later when Nike stepped in as part of a new design

that also saw the club crest positioned centrally on the shirt. But this deal was also to last only a single year as Nike, who had previously only had a deal with Sunderland, moved on to become the behemoth we see today and didn't need comic book sales to create real-world commercial traction.

In 1991 the kit was designed by a readership competition winner and a simple, classic combination of red and white was chosen. But this shirt was also to become home to SEGA, followed the next season by High Street bank TSB then Subbuteo until 1995. Two years later Melchester, now incorporated into the *Match of the Day* magazine, were sponsored by the show as part of a gaudy and Americanised design that you would expect to be paraded by Liverpool's friend Ronald McDonald. Partick Thistle were to go full Melchester with their 2017 kit's central red stripe dividing two panels of yellow topped by red shoulder panels and sleeves. The red socks with yellow trim completed a

smart and pleasing homage to Roy Race and his chums and is a kit design yet to be topped since.

In the 2000s, reflecting the times we live in, they were to be sponsored by those obesity generating giants McDonald's. There was something particularly dispiriting about that. It felt like they had betrayed Roy's Corinthian spirit in an increasingly desperate dash for cash. The pure values of Melchester's yellow and red had now been mortgaged and sullied by the same primary colours enticing children to drag their parents' wallets into a gaudy world of saturated fats and calorie-dense edible cardboard. Melchester's kits were a touchstone for how football culture had moved from wide-eyed innocence and commercially naive custodians to brutal commercialism and consumption. Unfortunately for Roy and his team-mates, they were singing songs of innocence and not experience. There would only be one winner.

Roy continues to hobble on (well you would with one foot) and

a website with plenty of 404 Not Found pages tries to fan the embers of interest. A new kit was released for the 2021/22 season described as 'a classic reimagined' which riffs on their 1973–78 kit above. Another impressive partnership is with Her Game Too official partners Hope and Glory Sportswear, who have not only produced a kit from recycled plastic (each shirt is made from 16 plastic bottles) but are ethics driven and community focussed: donating much of their profits – in the case of Her Game Too, all of them – to grassroots initiatives. In yet another blow to my bank balance, the design is also a beauty. With its single vertical yellow line on the left and yellow collar framing a red body, the Melchester Rovers tiger growling from the logo, *Roy of the Rovers* left sleeve and National Literacy Trust badge on the right, this is an achingly attractive throwback with a modern twist. A shirt designed to educate and escape instead of consume and suffer. Long live Roy Race.

Can Tracey Crouch Save our Shirts?

08

Two years in the making after the Conservative commitment made in 2019, Tracey Crouch's interim report, released in July 2021, shared the same values as a group I am proud to have worked for.

In my role as regional media manager for Fair Game, it gives me a real sense of pride to see how we all believe fans should be given the final say on any proposed change to a club's 'crown jewels', which includes the name, nickname, colours, badge and the geographical location of where they play. Although the phrase conjures up images of being in a defensive wall on a cold Sunday morning nursing a hangover and trying to protect the family version, it is a key plank in what we all, as fans, value.

Crouch described our approach as 'protecting heritage assets' and adopted a strident and uncompromising approach that gave us great hope:

'We have seen strong evidence that existing protections of key club heritage items of great cultural and emotional importance to fans is not sufficient. The most pressing of these has been the many clubs who appear to have lost the rights to their home grounds, but much evidence was also received of concerns relating to items such as club badges, location, colours and competitions.'

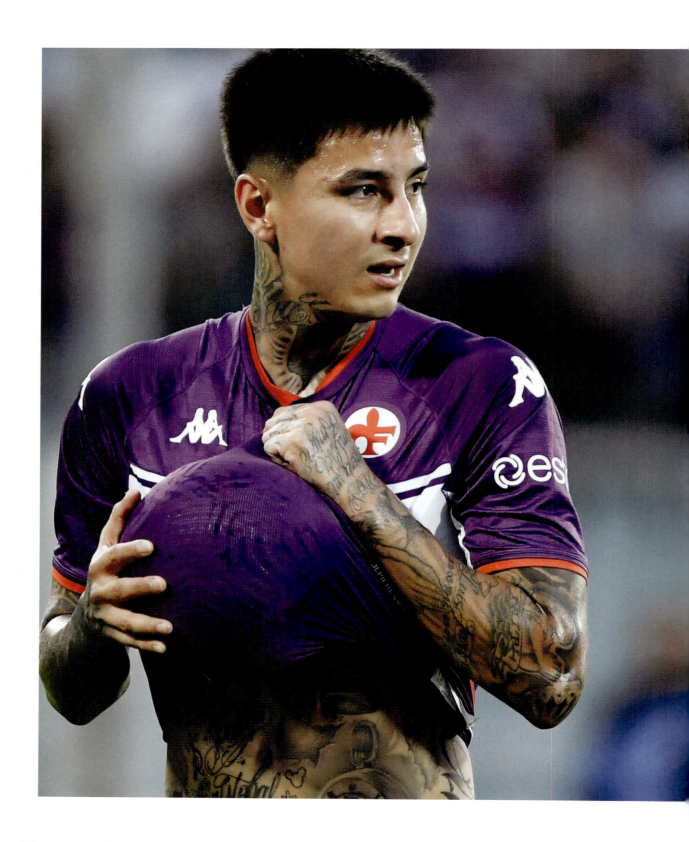

This paragraph was music to our Fair Game ears and gave us added momentum through the summer as we welcomed clubs, MPs and even town councils to our collective determination to preserve our heritage assets. A club crest has huge emotional currency for fans. It's a touchstone to tap into their club and family's history, a rallying point and, when kits change every five minutes, usually a comforting constant to cling on to in a frighteningly fast-moving world. That's why it is guarded so jealously. This was shown in sharp relief when, in late March 2022, Fiorentina decided to change their crest design with little fan consultation. The response was mixed, to say the least, with some supporters venting their displeasure by hanging a banner in front of the stadium reading, 'Before changing history, make it.'

Another fan cut to the heart of why a crest needs preservation over 'refreshing':

'This isn't American soccer but Italian football. Here it has a value, above all a symbol from the heart. No to the new logo.'

There are the sublime responses, but also the ridiculous – in March 2022, Manchester City issued a cease and desist warning to a Chilean third-tier outfit over similarities between the clubs' crests even though the South Americans had yet to play a professional game. City's nine-page document made it very clear how high their lawyers' hourly rate was and Santiago City, despite being so small that they don't have a Wikipedia page to share dodgy half-truths and run a Facebook page with a following of 75 (76 including me) felt the full legal force of City's legion of lawyers.

Surprisingly, considering the huge emotional response it generates we haven't seen them for long. As Routledge and Wills explain in their sumptuous book *The Beautiful Badge*, 'Even in the late 1960s, many clubs like Manchester United wore plain shirts, uncluttered by badges, logos and brands. There were no badges for the likes of Best, Law and Charlton to kiss except for special events such as the European Cup Final of 1968.'

This was something wistfully revisited on 10 February 2008 when, for the Manchester derby, both sides wore unbranded shirts to commemorate the 50th anniversary of the Munich air disaster.

Crest sacrilege

There is a sacrosanct feeling about crests as an oasis of purity on a shirt buffeted by commercial considerations. But that doesn't mean clubs have always been able to resist planting their sponsors' sticky fingers on them. Between 1976 and 1978 Borussia Dortmund decided to test the Bundesliga's resolve by teaming up with tobacco company Samson, with the cigarette makers not only shirt sponsors but part of the club's crest. This was a highly unpopular move with the fans, not helped by the club registering their record defeat, losing 12-0 at Borussia Mönchengladbach on 29 April 1978.

Tobacco companies had the financial muscle to sponsor clubs and even whole leagues when smoking was at its peak. Austria Vienna had Austria Tabak as their shirt sponsors from 1977 to 2004, promoting their main brand Memphis. The club were even renamed Austria Memphis in 1977, which would also last until 2004. In Colombia following the killing of a referee in 1989, Mustang cigarettes seemed to fit the profile of danger and possible death, so officials decided to rebrand the league the Copa Mustang.

But Dortmund weren't even the first German club to use their crest as just another sponsorship opportunity.

In 1972 Eintracht Braunschweig were, like many other German clubs, in financial trouble after the Bundesliga bribery scandal the previous year. To get out of the financial hole caused by the scandal Braunschweig called on alcoholic cough syrup giant Jägermeister for shirt sponsorship money. Nothing unusual about that nowadays, but putting an alcohol brand there went down badly with the men on Bundesliga committees and the plan was eventually scuppered. So, thought the club, if it can't go there, let's put it on the crest instead. As you can imagine, that went down like a Jägermeister on an empty stomach. In 1983 the club tried to rename itself 'Jägermeister Braunschweig' which also received short shrift from the authorities.

That bribery scandal in 1971 was astonishing: swathes of German matches were rigged and, in the fallout, 52 players (15 of whom played for Eintracht Braunschweig) and two managers were punished. But there was a strange twist for the Braunschweig players. They accepted payments, but not always to throw a game. They were at times also incentivised to try harder and win. In one game, incredibly, bribes were on the table from two sources. One for the team to win and one for them to throw the match.

On 5 June 1971, for the last game of the season, Hertha Berlin were at home to Arminia Bielefeld. Bielefeld, a point behind fellow strugglers Offenbach, needed to beat a Berlin side undefeated at home all season and 'hope' Offenbach would also lose. To seal the deal Bielefeld offered Hertha a quarter of a million Deutsche Marks to throw the game while Offenbach offered a mere 160,000 for them to win it. And this was where it got truly surreal. Hertha decided that, rather than accept the higher offer of throwing the game, they would end the season on a positive, take the lower bribe and make up the difference with a win bonus. Despite deciding this, they lost and Bielefeld assumed this was a conscious decision so, after the game, a briefcase full of cash was sent to the Hertha team. As you can imagine, shirt sponsorship to put your brand next to these shenanigans was thoroughly toxic.

Another unusual part of this episode for the Germans was their decision to put the club/Jägermeister logo in the centre of the shirt. Aston Villa's 2000/01 kit followed this approach and put both the logo and brand at the centre of the shirt, something they had done the season before. We are so used to having our crest above our hearts that it is easy to forget that shirts with a manufacturer's logo are a relatively recent addition. With our eyes seeking out the first piece of top-left information with our writing starting in the same format, the manufacturers preferred the right breast anyway. In 1976 the established manufacturers, Umbro and Bukta, introduced a new range of kits featuring their own logos incorporated into the trim on the sleeves, shorts and socks in the English game as well

as making sure their logos appeared prominently on the players' chests. The dam had now been opened.

Bizarrely, for the 1985 to 1987 kit, Villa kept up with the centralised sponsor's logo but dispensed with the club logo entirely. That must be the biggest crest sacrilege of all; something Puma hadn't considered in 2021 when their third kit designs for Manchester City, Milan, Marseille, Valencia, Fenerbahçe and Borussia Mönchengladbach came out crestfallen. Thanks to the amplifying power of social media, they were forced into an embarrassing u-turn with their Dortmund Champions League kit. Fans noticed, and were outraged by, their lack of crest in their victory over Beşiktaş on 15 September. So, for their game against Sporting Lisbon 13 days later, they wore a hurriedly redesigned shirt that welcomed back the crest. They won 1-0, so karma was restored.

Adidas would try their luck at leveraging fan loyalty for increased sales by producing their City Pack in May 2021. Perhaps they spent too long in the hermetically sealed environment of American franchise teams playing in protective leagues, but this does seem a tone-deaf attempt for fans to support the city and not their club. In Bucharest, Dinamo and Steaua supporters are surely not expected to lay down their colours (Steaua even have red and blue in their home kits like the City Pack) and follow their city. You have to admire the marketing spin for these, but surely they knew that, like the European Franchise League shirts, they are destined for a one-way trip across to wholesaleclearance.co.uk and they certainly won't be going for their original highly optimistic price point of £55:

> 'It's made from silky, dull-shine fabric for a classic look and feel. On the back, the flock-print number and name add a quality finish.'

A football shirt with a number on the back. Revolutionary.

When Tracey Crouch's final report came out on 24 November 2021, the 162 pages gave us all great hope that this would be the start of a more sustainable future for football. Although the report would only mention the 'heritage assets' three times, crouched (pun intended) in rather vague terms there was a commitment to 'look at interventions to protect club identity, including geographical location and historical features [e.g. club badges]'. There was more strident support, through the idea of a fan empowering 'Golden Share' to protect the club name after 90 per cent (over 17,000) respondents wanted the share to protect it against changes, 87 per cent supported it protecting a club's colours and 83 per cent wanted it to protect the club badge. A Golden Share leans towards trust-run clubs like Exeter City, where fans have the power to avoid another Wimbledon-style relocation, and there is clearly the subtext of

trying to ward off the next European Franchise League:

they are cleared of the nine Premier League gambling front-of-shirt sponsors

'The Golden Share would require the consent of the shareholder to certain actions by the club – specifically selling the club stadium or permanently relocating it outside of its local area, joining a new competition not affiliated to FIFA, UEFA and the FA, or changing the club badge, the club name or first team home colours.'

Crouch put some meat on to the bones of her ideas when asked to appear in front of the Digital, Culture, Media and Sport Committee on 7 December that year. Supported by a positive and collegial set of questions in an arena that has often been hostile, Crouch described the heritage assets that shirts are part of as a package of measures to enfranchise fans, 'To be able to have a say over matters of heritage. For example, so they wouldn't be able to move around the country like we saw with Wimbledon going to Milton Keynes. I think this is a holistic package which protects English football.'

Gary Neville, speaking passionately later that day on Sky Sports, showed he was all in on the idea of protecting the images that describe our footballing fandoms, 'They are heritage assets: football clubs that actually people live their lives for every single week, so for me I think that it's a great opportunity to reset English football.'

Going forward, shirts will measure the success of the Crouch report. If

and companies funnelling finance via Malta, the Caribbean and the Isle of Man then we will know which way the tide is turning. For the sake of all our footballing futures, we can only hope that we will be wearing shirts that make us proud not only of our club, but the game we all love. The alternative, as Cardiff City showed, would be unbearable to contemplate for us 'legacy fans'.

Cardiff fans had already been warned at the turn of the new millennium. After taking over, Sam Hammam astonishingly (especially to Swansea, Newport and Wrexham fans) proclaimed that the whole Welsh nation would support the club that he was now renaming the 'Cardiff Celts'. Oh, and by the way, their kits would now be green, red and white. He rolled back on the name idea after a post-decision discussion with players reminiscent of boxing promoter Bob Arum's philosophy that negotiations only really start after a contract has been signed. While Hammam couldn't

resist tinkering with the crest, it still contained the acceptable elements of the bluebird, Welsh flag and the club's nickname. His fingers had been burned and, duly chastised, he (almost) learnt his lesson. Would he have faced so much opprobrium if he was British? Possibly not, but misreading the football cultural currents is not the preserve of billionaire foreign owners. At Newcastle United, Freddie Shepherd and Douglas Hall were stung by the *News of the World*'s 'Fake Sheik' in March 1998 making fun of fans paying over the odds for kits. As Tom Bower describes it in *Broken Dreams*:

'On the tape, recorded by the *News of the World* they had talked about their sexual conquests, describing Newcastle girls as "ugly dogs", and boasting about their club's sale of shirts to fans for £50 which cost £5 to manufacture.'[7]

[7] Bower, T., *Broken Dreams* (Simon & Schuster UK, Kindle edition)

The hatred for Blackpool chairman Karl Oyston, which led to a long-running and mutually damaging boycott by the vast majority of Tangerines fans, only recently ended in victory for the long-suffering supporters. But Cardiff owner Tan's tone-deaf decisions created huge unease in fans of a club steeped in history, if not success. In 2012 Tan clearly hadn't read the memo or reflected on recent history, despite having had two years in control of the club to immerse himself in what sustains football fan culture. The

Malaysian decided a change from the blue that Bluebirds had worn for over a century to red would bring the luck many in south-east Asia believe the colour represents. This desire was spun by the Malaysian owners as a way to expand City's international appeal.

The plan was to slide this change under the door while promised stadium and training centre investment on condition of their compliance with the kit change slipped through the letterbox. Bad mistake. Being sponsored by a country two years later was another discombobulating adaptation for a fanbase previously wearing shirts promoting Vans Direct and Redrow Homes. What Tan did not understand was how football culture accepts a nudge in one direction, but when that nudge becomes an elbow to the face, there is a deep well of historical resentment ready to be rolled out. All this even though the 'Redbirds' (as no one was calling them) were to top the Championship and fly fleetingly to the Premier League before being brutally shot down a year later. If the club you own won the Championship by eight points and you are still largely reviled by your fanbase, it must be tempting to reflect that you should have left their kit well alone.

Cardiff's chief executive at the time, Alan Whiteley, was testing the tensile strength of the rope he was soon to be hung with when, through gritted teeth and tin hat standing by, he told the BBC:

'The change of colour is a radical and some would say revolutionary move which will be met with unease and apprehension by several supporters, along with being seen as controversial by many.'

The kit change was to last for three turbulent years before Tan folded in a bid to 'unite' the club. An interesting logic. Standing outside the fan culture that sees kits simply as revenue generators badly underestimates how much symbolic resonance they hold. Players who give less than 100 per cent for the club are 'not fit to wear the shirt'; players who kiss the club badge in celebration had better not push for the exit door like Villa's Fabian Delph. In July 2015, Delph signed for Manchester City just six days after saying he would be staying at Aston Villa to captain them into the next season and, when Steven Gerrard was flirting with Chelsea in 2005, burning shirts with his name on was the way Liverpool fans showed the heat of their anger.

Shirts are a yardstick for the weight of history in British football. In my 16 years living in Thailand, the football clubs are in their relative infancy. Changing kits, stadiums and even provinces does not cause widespread fan unrest. The through thread of intergenerational support has yet to be spun out, so change is more part of settling than a destabilising force. Perhaps Tan would have been advised to adopt Granny's mantra. We have two ears and one mouth so we can listen twice as much as we speak.

'09

#prayforneymar

Working in Thai football was, particularly for the first two years, a thankless task. I tried to explain that a media offering in English would help clubs gain a bigger global audience, add to their shirt sales and support their push for the Thai Premier League (as it was called in those days) to be the dominant force in south-east Asia.

My pitches were often met with confused incredulity which ran something along the lines of, 'But we are Thai. Why do we need to use English?' While fighting against this soul-destroying tidal wave of apathy I used to regularly meet up for a coffee with friend and *L'Équipe* photographer Pascal Della Zuana. He would jet around the world recording big tennis tournaments, Formula 1 and, occasionally, football. He

would also help me drum up support by photographing meetings with people such as England and Manchester United legend Bryan Robson.

By 2014 I finally secured a job in the Bangkok province of Suphanburi, owned by an Anglophile president and now a Thai cabinet minister. When Pascal and I met before he flew off to cover the World Cup in his home country of Brazil, I tried to persuade him to take my

Suphanburi FC baseball cap around the various World Cup stadiums and photograph them in what, on reflection, was a pretty lame attempt to create a 'Suphanburi World Cap 2014'. Luckily, Pascal agreed to take the cap but refused to take any photos. On his return, we met again in our usual Amazon Coffee stall at the ostentatious Paragon Shopping Mall in downtown Bangkok and he told me the story of the infamous night in Belo Horizonte when Brazil were steamrollered 7-1.

Pascal had access to the Brazilian changing room before the game as part of a select group of international journalists. To the amazement of them all, the Brazilian team decided to honour their absent brother Neymar Junior, who had, for once in the tournament, rolled along the floor with an actual injury in the quarter-final against Colombia. The Brazilian squad, famed for their religious fervour that regularly got in the way of training sessions when it clashed with church services, decided to create a shrine to Neymar. They formed a circle around Neymar's shirt and prayed to it. One of Pascal's colleagues looked at the unfurling deification and told him there was no point in staying for the game. Brazil had no chance of beating the uber-efficient Germans if their pre-match warm-up was a church service commemorating a player with a back injury and left the changing room then stadium.

After it was seriously prayed to, we fans saw the shirt again before the game. It looked like a gesture of solidarity with a stricken team-mate. What we didn't realise was that it was in fact a religious artefact. You can see in David Luiz's face that the very last thing on his mind is the upcoming game; one that commentator Alan Hansen described as 'one of the worst performances I have ever seen'. And so, the shirt that was supposed to inspire brought about one of the most humiliating 29 minutes in Brazilian footballing history.

With an hour to go they were five down and, unlike Neymar's shirt, they didn't have a prayer.

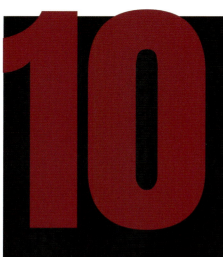

10 St. Pauli

Football's Counter Culture Club

Let's face it, German club St. Pauli are just plain different. The club's nickname fits their disparate but committed global fanbase: *Freibeuter der Liga* (the League's Freebooters) and their logo may seem to be traditional northern German symbolism, but its motto continues the reactionary theme, 'Non established since 1910'.

Adding to the heady carnival of causes at the Millerntor-Stadion is the regular appearance of the Jolly Roger. In happy times, it symbolises the ethically conscious, ragtag collection of Social Romantics (originally a pejorative term for a group determined to lobby against the club's increasing commercialism) but when the fans want to vent their anger at the club's decisions, the Jolly Roger Rouge appears: the flag used by pirates to warn that no quarter or prisoners would be taken or given. In

England, Manchester City fans started a craze of bringing huge inflatable bananas to games as a surreal gesture towards that often socially grim 1980s decade. English football was banned from Europe, beset with hooliganism, and threatened with a national ID card but St. Pauli used the skull and crossbones as a middle-fingered salute to the footballing and business establishment. The flag became the unofficial club logo for fans, and, in the 2015/16 season, Hummel's kit design added a twist that not only promoted the pirates' calling card but flagged the club's heartfelt rather than bandwagon-jumping commitment to LGBT+ inclusion by adding rainbow-coloured skull and crossbones to the shirt.

Looking through the club's merchandise offerings this morning, two things stand out. The first is the

price of kits. The away shirt is just shy of €40 whereas, with fellow 2. Bundesliga team and historic foes Hamburg SV, you only get five cents in change from €90. What also stands out is how much of the merchandise has a campaigning angle. Coming from a Premier League universe where 'presentation' and 'anthem' jackets are pushed as a must-have add-on to the other non-necessities this is a Jutland Peninsula breath of fresh, cold air. Although caught between a corporate rock and a campaigning hard place, the club is not paying the standard tax-deductible lip service for corporate and social responsibility. This fight for fairness and creating a welcoming club environment for everyone is deep within their DNA. In the sparsely populated club trophy room, a poster tells us all we need to know about the club's values:

'We don't have silverware. Instead, we have something a lot better. We have a story to tell. The incredible story of how a community-based club from Hamburg becomes one of the most famous football teams in Europe. Without big trophies. Without big money.'

There is something refreshingly, joyously bonkers about the 2. Bundesliga club located in Hamburg's red light district. They are an oasis of subversive sanity (or infectious insanity) in the monetised footballing universe around it of corporate behemoths

KIT&**CABOODLE**

driving 'brand value' and 'global profile' while relentlessly data-mining fans like a footballing Facebook. In 2011's *FC St. Pauli: A Socialist Football Club in Hamburg's Red Light District*, author Marcel Theroux described them as, 'a tiny ship of pirates in a sea of commercialism'. But German branding expert Oliver Kaiser of the Ledavi agency is depressingly perceptive as he looks to the data-driven future of fandom:

'The intelligent club in the future will say, "Well, company, you want to have my 25 million fans. I don't give it to you. It's mine." The company will have to fork out. A database of 25 million fans could be worth billions.'

Uncoupled from the prevailing culture of what Paul Nicholson, in his excellent and eviscerating book *Can We Have our Football Back?*, called 'genuflecting at the feet of Mammon' the club consistently operates on first principles. For me, any club whose theme tune as the players enter the pitch is 'Hell's Bells' already has my attention.

They certainly do things a little differently around the club described by Nilsson in his glorious *World Football*

Club Crests as 'amid castles, skulls and whorehouses'. Take the 2006 FIFI Wild Cup, a tournament where countries not recognised by FIFA got a chance to share the spotlight. Greenland, Tibet and Zanzibar made up half of the territories represented, while St. Pauli proudly represented the 'Republic of St. Pauli'. When I thought I couldn't love them more, they came fourth, and as for their national flag – it could only be the Jolly Roger. Oh, and the FIFI Wild Cup began with the cry of 'This is a Sepp Blatter-free zone!' But the tournament highlighted the club's financial tightrope. As club president Oke Göttlich told BBC reporter Harry Poole,

'We definitely need to aim for higher goals … We're trying to find the right balance between our values and the need to be tough, structured and organised as a football club.'

A well-meaning tournament trying to give those outside the FIFA universe a platform was sponsored by a group of online gambling companies, challenging the genuine desire to see a fairer footballing universe and a catch-22 agreement for the club that would otherwise not have been able to host the event. Despite the attraction of watching Zanzibar beat Greenland 4-2, there were very few fans to witness it and the Wild Cup faded into loss-making obscurity, leaving Northern Cyprus with the bragging rights as champions, possibly for eternity.

A decade ago, St. Pauli decided to share a core set of 'Guiding Principles'. What gives them teeth is the way they were embedded not only in their intentions and behaviours, but for every action the club took going forward. As the club related, 'These principles will form an integral part of contracts and agreements in future and serve as a reference point for everyone involved with the club.'

This approach is likely to give some sponsors concern. Despite announcing a partnership with Jack Daniel's in the 2019/20 season, they refused to allow their logo on the shirt. This was an understandable decision for a club determined to connect with only local businesses, but the whisky had already been front and centre of their kits from 1997 and the logo would, in the new deal, still be seen on the team bus and in social media.

Something else to give the sponsors pause is this section of the principles:

'Sponsors and commercial partners of FC St. Pauli and its products should be in accord with the social and political responsibility of the club.'

One of the key tenets is being driven by the will of the fans, which can cause income streams to dry up in our world of constant media and brand bombardment. When beggars are choosers, those they reject could be the ones with the deepest pockets. It was the fans who vetoed selling stadium naming rights to a sponsor and pre-match minutes are commercial-free to allow fans full voice. Even for a League Two club like Exeter City, this precious pre-match platform allows them to generate much-needed revenue as one of the country's few fan-owned clubs who are forced to run off financial fumes. How else would lucky Devonian fans be able to connect with Carpetright, Thatchers Cider and RGB Building Supplies?

In the brutal, cold calculations of a cost/benefit analysis, principles often make supply chain demands they are not used to:

'The sale of goods and services at FC St. Pauli is driven not only by commercial considerations but also by the principles of social compatibility, diversified offering, sustainability and ecology.'

What would energise and inspire these fans in search of a club worthy of their support was how the principles extended way beyond the pitch, regularly referring to how their non-negotiable goals extended 'beyond the sphere of sport'. Fans are part of something bigger. The club, through these explicitly stated principles, is determined to be a 'symbol of sporting authenticity' irrespective of what

10 St Pauli. Football's Counter Culture Club

111

happens on the pitch. Some would say despite it. Only eight of their 110 years have been spent in the top Bundesliga and only one season has been spent there in almost the last two decades. Hoping to celebrate their 70th 'non established' anniversary in 1980, instead, they were faced by club sponsors embarrassed to be connected to them and determined to sever all links. So much so that the players were forced to play with shirts that amateurishly patched over their previous paymasters' logos. Although a moment of dark despair, it was a watershed that started a fan-generated and socially conscious club with a rambunctious and disparately driven determination to take on 'a world dominated by power and not love'.

This gave the club a chance to use the shirt as a focal point for a new set of aspirations. Fans driven out of rivals Hamburg SV by far-right terrace brutes could show how, as Nick Davidson describes it in *Pirates, Punks & Politics: FC. St. Pauli – Falling in Love with a Radical Football Club*, anyone lucky enough 'to wear that shirt knows that you don't just represent a football club, you represent a community, a political movement, a religion'.

The principles underscoring this new sense of community give a nod to the need for a commercial profile, but only if it is part of the fans' behaviour, 'The active fanbase [i.e. primarily those actively involved on matchday] are the foundation for the

emotionalisation of football, which in turn constitutes the basis for the marketability of FC St. Pauli.'

Talking to the BBC's Harry Poole, Michael Pahl, chair of the club's fan-founded museum, added:

'St. Pauli is about authenticity. It's about doing things differently, finding your own way and staying true to your values as much as possible in a very commercialised environment.'

Poole was enchanted by his dealings with the club. Writing in June 2020, he described St. Pauli as 'Hamburg's unapologetically political team'. Even though they had narrowly avoided relegation to Germany's third tier, their merchandise and ticket sales were bested by only three of the country's biggest clubs. Pre-pandemic, matchday tickets were rare commodities. Like Sunderland in their continuing League One slump whose home attendances in the 2019/20 season made up a staggering sixth of the total crowds for the division. Averaging an eye-watering 31,327 foul-weather supporters subjected to dire games in a majestic Stadium of Light, the match was only part of the story. Two decades before this constitutional bill of rights, St. Pauli had been just another club, but fans sick of that far-right vitriol of some of the neighbouring Hamburg fans needed a focus for fighting their revulsion and St. Pauli provided it. As Nilsson continued, 'Awareness of the club's anti-fascism and social activism spread, and in the space of only a couple of years the stands that had previously held perhaps a thousand fans were now packed. For a long time, St. Pauli was a club like so many others, but in the early '80s they achieved cult status.'

Talking on Sho TV's 2011 documentary, *Paulinen Platz*, head of Upsolut Merchandising Hendrik Luttner emphasised how, for this club, selling kits is not important. What a beautiful, bonkers approach to business when other clubs are ramming shirt sale units down our throats to help them leverage the next multimillion-pound kit deal. For him, shoulder-shruggingly:

'Selling football jerseys? Yes. A very typical question for St. Pauli as it is an untypical football club. I think we sell about 15,000 to 25,000 a year depending on second or first division. It's not as many as other clubs but the jersey is not that important, it's our decision whether it's sold out or not. We could produce it for the whole season. A jersey represents the football: the crossbones symbol represents everything around the club and football also. That makes it a bit more interesting for a lot of people who are not only trying to wear football jerseys; it is unusual, but you can't copy it. It's very special.'

To be even more attractively contrary, the kit deal signed in 2016 with Under Armour went down badly with a section of the St. Pauli fans because of their range including hunting gear and their connections with the US military. The company had to go on a charm offensive and contribute to local Hamburg charities to guide the agreement through. That deal came to an end in 2021 and, in delightfully typical St. Pauli style, their new kits were made in house using the logo DIIY. As you would expect, the kits focus on fair trade, sustainability, and transparency.

Another German club took partnership and sustainability a step further. The Bundesliga's TSG Hoffenheim played against VfL Bochum on 2 April 2022 wearing a shirt celebrating 'Africa Matchday'. The club has its own sustainable clothing brand, Umoja, which was featured on the shirt front after the main sponsor – business management software company SAP – stepped aside. Swahili for 'unity', 20 per cent of Umoja shirt sales and money generated from an auction of match-worn shirts were given to club charity partner Viva con Agua for the Football4Wash project in Uganda, where the club merchandise is produced. This model of supporting charities not only by offering money but empowering and enfranchising the supply chain to source, refine and produce stands as a case study in how to share not only funds but skills, experience, employment and sustainability. Produced in safe and inspected working conditions using sustainably sourced materials, there were only 1,000 shirts made that not only riff on an elegant African style, but speak to what the wearer and

KIT&**CABOODLE**

club values. The match shirts act as invitations to engage with the rest of the brand's range that drives fairer, safer working conditions that are rewarded with a wage that helps them build healthier families. A superb, joined-up approach was summarised in their club press release as:

proudly proclaimed '*Kein Fussball den Faschisten*' (no football for the fascists).

Later we visit League Two's Forest Green Rovers, England's proto St. Pauli. Harry Poole was also inspired by the German club's determination, like Forest to present 'a window on a more sustainable future in the modern game'.

> 'We want to awaken a sense of responsibility. At the same time, we want to strengthen socially and ecologically sustainable development. There and here.'

Club president Oke Göttlich explained at their kit launch, 'Not only, but in particular, during the crisis posed by Covid-19, we are striving to meet the challenges with courage and entrepreneurial spirit along with all St. Pauli fans. This independence, and the search for new avenues, has always been a hallmark of FC St. Pauli. In launching our own teamsport collection, we remain steadfastly on our path of independence. The strength of a member-run club is reflected in the implementation of our members' ideas. In this way, we can face any crisis together. DIIY, incidentally, is derived from the term DIY, or do it yourself. That's exactly what FC St. Pauli is all about – not just moaning but doing it better yourself.'

Of course, this being St. Pauli, for the last game of the season they dispensed with their shirt sponsor for an anti-fascist limited edition which

In sleepy Gloucestershire, the strident rallying cry is front and centre of their stylish website, 'Sustainability is central to everything we do at Forest Green Rovers. From solar panels and electric vehicle charging points at the New Lawn, to our vegan matchday menu, we strive to be the greenest football club in the world.'

In our football world of global online footprints and marketing spin doctors, there is something deeply satisfying about how St. Pauli simply stumbled on their new identity driven by the collective will of their fans almost a century into the club's existence. As Poole described it affectionately:

'There was no grand plan when a supporter from the local *Hafenstrasse* squats defiantly waved a pirate flag on the terraces as a light-hearted representation of poor St. Pauli taking on the rich. But it was then that St. Pauli was adopted as a footballing home for those seeking a different way.'

For Forest Green Rovers, owner Dale Vince only became involved when, as he told FIFA TV:

'Forest Green is our local club and in the summer of 2010 was in some trouble … financially. The guys here asked me to come up and watch a game and I met them. It was a lovely place. They said, "We just need a bit of money to get through to the summer," and that was the beginning.'

Despite the constant struggles to stand for something, St. Pauli hopes that the current pandemic will help fans move away from the monied behemoths at the top of the game and reassess what football means to their community. Oke Göttlich agrees with John Nicholson's brutal contention that, 'The beating dark heart of the Premier League is the sulphurous devil that is money.'

Göttlich's perspective is less acerbic but just as heartfelt:

'There is so much money involved now that we are forced to play games for TV and not for the fans. This is really bad because football was always for the spectators and the people and it brings togetherness. If you are a community-based club taking care of your region then a game without fans is a nightmare.'

He and Nicholson are clearly soul mates. In return, Nicholson describes how, 'They have taken television from being a guest at football to football being a guest on television.'

It's easy to agree with Nicholson, but hard not to empathise with Göttlich who speaks for so many of us feeling disenfranchised by paywalls and the atomisation of access to the clubs we love through multiple subscriptions offering financial death by a thousand cuts. 'I really hope – and this is where I am a romantic and a fighter for community-based football – that we can create a model for competitive integrity, to create a level playing field and think in new ways.'

Long live the people's Freebooters!

Back in England, Southend's very own St. Pauli On Sea keeps the rainbow flag flying for their German namesakes not only with a charity team but a range of merchandise that supports Football Versus Homophobia. Kieran Casey's outstanding Sartorial Soccer ('memories are made of polyester') describes them as, 'positive rebels' who use their kits designed by Kit and Bone as a reimagining of their parent club's inclusive and iconoclastic approach. Kieran spoke to designer Matt about the attraction of creating a shirt that spoke of what both the German and Essex clubs stand for.

Matt responded, 'The club's "positive rebel" stance has always resonated with us and the way we work at Kit and Bone, so having a chance to put our creative take on the club's iconic colours and style for this group of fans was brilliant.'

The shirt Matt helped design will give £5 from each sale to local homeless charity Harp. A little piece of the Millerntor-Stadion is fighting for the ones left behind in south Essex.

Message Received?

Shirts can be the ideal platform for more explicit communication with the fans, but what they are trying to say is not always exactly clear.

It's 1995 and, as Roma and Inter Milan prepare for another match in front of incendiary fans, they decide to make a stand against the previous toxic atmosphere between the two sets of Ultras by deciding to play in the wrong combination of kits. Half was their own and the other of their opposition. You have to recognise their well-meaning attempt, but beyond them looking plain odd, it's hard to imagine any fan reflecting on and changing their behaviour after seeing the players exchange quirky kit combinations.

A much clearer Serie A message was made in November 2021. Commemorating the first anniversary of their favourite son's death, Napoli played three matches in a shirt featuring the image of Maradona. His storied seven years after joining from Barcelona in 1984 created a special bond with the club that, with his shirt image covered in a fingerprint, suggests he is now part of Napoli's DNA when they play at their Stadio Diego Armando Maradona. Having said that, by late November this was to be their tenth shirt of the season.

That is just plain bonkers, but they weren't done yet. In late January 2022 they released their 11th official third shirt in the 2021/22 season and by 2 March had gone on to produce four Maradona shirts and 13 for the season. Please make them stop.

Some clubs move from shirts as a commemoration to catalysts for social justice. In Brazil, Corinthians wore shirts with political and social messages. Looking to encourage people to vote in the election for governor of São Paulo on 15 March 1983, the kit carried the message '*Dia 15 Vote*' ('Vote on the 15th'). They would also play with the phrase '*Ganhar ou perder, mas sempre com democracia*' ('Win or lose, but always in democracy') to show exactly what they and their club stood for. Much of the drive for creating a club with a clear philosophy came from Sócrates Brasileiro Sampaio de Souza Vieira de Oliveira. As plain old Sócrates he explained to his biographer, Andrew Downie, 'Football came by accident. I was more interested in politics. I always had my eyes turned to the social injustices in the country. I just happened to be good at football, which gave me entrance to a very different and privileged environment … If people do not have the power to say things, then I will say it for them.'

Using the iconic shirts as a canvas to promote the power of the ballot box over the bullwhip stands in stark contrast to their 1986 World Cup design that sneakily used the sacred space of the national logo to promote Brazilian coffee wholesalers Café do Brasil. This sullies the shirt and betrays the tradition it represents, but wasn't as embarrassingly clunky as their effort in the 1962 tournament where, during the coin toss, the match ball sat incongruously on top of a sack of Brazilian coffee. It made the Volkswagen-branded remote control cars bringing the match balls on to the pitch in the 2020 Euros look almost, almost classy.

If you have a strong culture to share, your shirt is the perfect catalyst for promoting a philosophy. In this Premier League era shirt billboards share important messages like Black Lives Matter but also myriad invitations to consume, gamble and overspend. So it is easy to forget just what a risk these Brazilians were taking towards the end of the last century. English protests against odious absentee landlord owners may result in a fine or viral online infamy but going against the Brazilian junta could have deadly results for the players and their families. That was why their decision to play a game in 1982 with the demand 'I Want to Vote for My President' printed on their backs, in explicit defiance of the regime, showed incredible bravery. Four years later in the 1986 World Cup, Sócrates would often play wearing a headband sharing a political message. The US had controversially bombed Libya that summer. Sócrates's response was the declaration 'Yes to Love, No to Terror' on his head.

KIT&**CABOODLE**

In his excellent book *St. Pauli: Another Football is Possible*, Carles Viñas touches on Corinthians as St. Pauli's soulmates. In 1910 a group of railway workers drew inspiration from the English Corinthians founded a century before. But fast forward seven decades and the club based on the first principles of 'sportsmanship, fair play, [and] playing for the love of the game' played against a backdrop of brutal military dictatorship. Corinthians Paulista was in an existential crisis. But rather than giving lip service to a philosophy with jingles on shirts, Sócrates led a movement to revolutionise the way this club was run. Instead of a top-down bored billionaire plaything approach, this would be management from the bottom up.

The shirts were their calling cards and calls to arms. One of the key concepts of this democratic revolution in a country ruled by despots went even further than the highly admired German 50 plus one philosophy. Instead of using suicidal Premier League leveraged debt-based buyouts, the club would be seen as a non-profit organisation with a philosophy of one person, one share and one vote. This would strengthen connections with their local community and focus on key points such as affordable ticket prices. The nearest model we have in England is the trust-run clubs like Exeter City who, for a minimum contribution of £2 a month, make you part of a highly attractive, inclusive philosophy as described by the club in their marketing pitch:

'For years, members of the trust have ensured the club's financial sustainability and ethical ethos, including the development of young footballers through our academy system. The trust, through a genuine commitment to progress through member engagement we ensure that the club is fully focused on its members, supporters and the local community.'

For Corinthians, democracy's 1985 arrival in Brazil brought an end to their hearts and minds campaign. Their icon Sócrates would move to Italy and sign for Fiorentina and the former directors moved back into the club. In a stunning move, Sócrates would wear the green and gold one more time in November 2004. However, at the ripe old age of 50, he wasn't having a final encore across a Brazilian pitch but instead coming on as a 78th-minute substitute for Garforth Town against Tadcaster. Persuaded to sign by the owner of a chain of Brazilian soccer schools, Sócrates typically asked for no fee other than a plane ticket. But Garforth on a freezing afternoon and this Brazilian legend were not a great mix. When he was asked to warm up, rather than stretching on the sideline, he assumed this meant going back to the changing room for a warm, a beer and a cigarette. He barely made it to the end of the game and, even though the team were sponsored by Lego, everything most certainly was not awesome with his fitness. But his touch and style never left him, even though his next appearances were cancelled by football's infamous 'mutual consent'.

Six years later, in a touching karmic finale, Sócrates was to die on 4 December 2011, the day Corinthians became Brazilian champions, fulfilling a lifelong dream:

'I want to die on a Sunday, with Corinthians as champions.'

Just when I thought the arrival of Sócrates to West Yorkshire couldn't be topped, in late January 2022 the Bull in the Barne pub team from Shropshire won an eBay competition to field fellow Brazilian legend Roberto Carlos as a substitute at one of their Shrewsbury & District games the following month.

At the time, Bull in the Barne were fifth in Division One of the Shrewsbury and District Sunday League, so late free kicks near the edge of the area seemed destined for only one player. Carlos released the kind of copy and paste statement shared on transfer deadline days, but this one praised a team he (and we) had never heard of that are based 50 miles away from a club he didn't sign for:

The 48-year-old was to play for only nine minutes in central midfield but managed to score a penalty before hobbling back to the touchline to nurse his aching knees. Despite that, they were to lose 4-3 to the mighty Harlescott Rangers, but internet gold was created later when, sharing beers with his team-mates back at the pub, Carlos picked up a FaceTime call from Sergio Ramos.

The Corinthian spirit may have been brutalised by the stampede to commercialisation, but English and Scottish trust-run clubs, the German 50 plus one model and fan-run clubs such as Hearts and Newport County set up as an antidote to Manchester United's Glazer regime keep a flickering flame of hope burning. Shirts hold the memories far longer than the sponsors plastered over them. They have the power to share a more meaningful message than spend, spend, spend and, occasionally some teams like Arsenal's No More Red anti-knife crime shirt show us there is another way.

'I'm excited to play for Bull in the Barne in Shrewsbury, paying homage to when I nearly signed for Birmingham City in the '90s, which is very close by.'

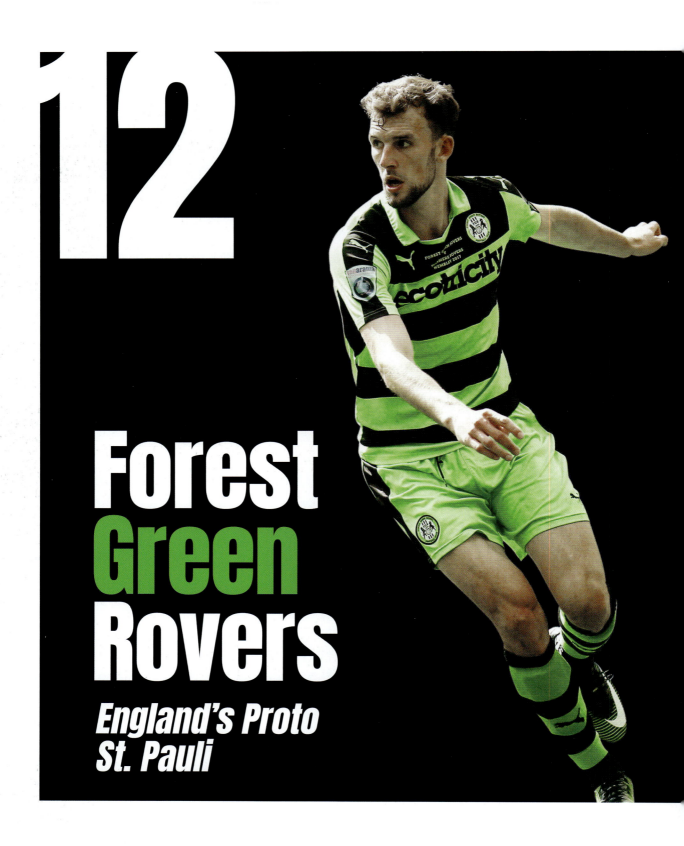

12

Forest Green Rovers

England's Proto St. Pauli

In January, Umbro announced that, for the 2023 season, League of Ireland side St Patrick's Athletic would wear shirts made with recycled polyester fabric taken from recycled plastic bottles.

In 2016 Adidas launched a range of kits made from ocean plastic for Real Madrid and Bayern Munich, as part of its partnership with marine conservation group Parley for the Oceans, and there has been a growing range of clubs taking this sustainable decision. In early February 2022 Puma launched the away kit of Brazilian Serie A side Palmeiras with a strong sustainability message that tied into the club's 'For a Greener Future' campaign. As Soccerbible described it:

'The jersey is constructed of raw yarn, using a Puma process called "Bye Dye", which reduces water consumption. The main colour of the jersey is the natural colour of yarn and on its front, the phrase "*Por um futuro mais verde*" (For a greener future) appears in a sublimated print.'

For many clubs, the kits are one idea in manifestos that don't address deeper issues of harmful, unsustainable practices in football. But, for one club, their kits are just one element in a culture that is all in on saving the environment of the game and the planet.

Culture is often defined as 'how we do things around here' and there are few better illustrations of this philosophy than the one nestled in the sleepy village of Nailsworth in Gloucestershire.

Forest Green Rovers' claim to be the 'World's Greenest Football Club' is like describing themselves as 'even more popular than Prince Andrew' or 'the winner in a competitive Russian election' but it's bold and speaks to what owner Dale Vince stands for. Writing in Steve Fleming's thought-provoking *Radical Football: Jürgen Griesbeck and the Story of Football for Good*, Vince's approach to sustainability is uncompromising and clear:

'You need to change the fundamentals of your organisation. Make the environment of equal importance to whatever your main purpose is. Put the environment into all of your thinking and decision-making. Start at the core. Change your DNA.'

The 2021 kit, a Hull-City-if-tigers-were-green look, is an acquired taste but, like St. Pauli, represents their guiding principles. It's made, wait for it, from bamboo. Slightly disingenuously when we look beneath the headlines,

[8] Fleming, S., *Radical Football: Jürgen Griesbeck and the Story of Football for Good*, p58 (Pitch Publishing, Kindle edition)

it is only a 50-50 mix with plastic but is streets ahead of most other clubs.

Their media copy describes the away kit as 'adopting a black-on-black zebra look'. A black on black zebra? That would be a dark horse then. There's also an unusual piece of innovation that courts internet controversy. The club started their non-league days with three stars on the shirt's back. Most clubs use stars to signify a league title or even a group of ten achieved, but for FGR they are a statement of intent. Each one plots their plan to reach the Championship, with the first one filled in to mark making it to League Two in 2017. It could be described as arriviste arrogance, but this is not a club projecting games at Old Trafford but potentially realistic second-tier football for someone with deep pockets and a ferocious drive like Vince.

Forest Green's kit also shares a similarity with St. Pauli's. The club's conservation partner, Sea Shepherd, is profiled on the base of the shirt's back using its skull and crossbones logo. Sea Shepherd shares Vince's philosophy: direct action and conservation through intervention rather than pleading. Apart from the 'black-on-black' away kit there is, of course, the third design. Just what a League Two team needs for those midweek Champions League games. To be fair, the design reflects the camouflage colour scheme on Sea Shepherd's flagship vessel the *Steve Irwin* and all sales of the kit (which will be worn in cup matches) will go directly to Sea Shepherd.

Another connection to St. Pauli comes from Roderick Bradley, founder of FGR kit maker PlayerLayer. Among the understandable media spin, there can't be many clubs apart from these two being described as 'rebellious' at a kit launch, as Bradley explained:

'We are privileged to work with such a forward-thinking, creative and rebellious football club. We are developing some completely natural fabrics which will change the sports clothing industry forever.'

The other end of the rebellious kit launch scale came in January 2022 when Chelsea launched a pre-match shirt. The excuse was to celebrate a decade since Chelsea won the Champions League in 2012, but there's flimsy and then there's wafer-thin.

Forest Green have embedded their guiding culture into the design, manufacture and sales of their shirts. They represent their mission statement that cascades down through every other aspect of the organisation. Described as a completely vegan football club, some of the players failed to get the memo in 2016 when they visited the local Greggs pasty shop and shot to fame thanks to its appearance on *Have I Got News For You*. But, as Barack Obama describes in his perceptive autobiography *The Promised Land*, 'Plan beats no plan.'

KIT&**CABOODLE**

Another key signature move was the world's first almost entirely wooden stadium finally getting green-lit after years of local council wrangling, with some members still aiming to appeal the decision even by the time of publication. This would give the club an infrastructure to supercharge its green mission. The latest plans, shared by Vince at the end of January 2022, included a hotel, business park, green tech business park and even provision for sheltered housing. Eco Park would be part of what many people see as Ecotricity Town. When *The Independent* interviewed Vince in 2014, journalist Tom Pilston noticed how much profile the company had in the local area, 'Get off the train at Stroud and the first building on the left is Ecotricity. Walk up to the main street, and the office block on the right is Ecotricity. On the outskirts of town, there is another one for Ecotricity. In fact, go anywhere in this part of Gloucestershire and it's impossible to avoid the renewable-energy company.'

With a population of only 2,000, making them the club from the smallest town in the Football League, it is trying to punch well above its weight when powered by Ecotricity.

Forest Green has been able to sustain its ties with sustainability through its choice of sponsors and business partners. While St. Pauli currently need to take in the euro of Jack Daniel's, betting company bwin and Astra beer, all of FGR's sponsors share the same or similar

values to the club. Whether it's Vince's Ecotricity, stadium naming rights holders Innocent Smoothies, or Quorn, the club has the same philosophy wherever you look. Even their address feeds into the same philosophy:

The Innocent New Lawn
Another Way
Nailsworth

While St. Pauli devised a list of five wide-ranging principles, Forest Green have a more specific club culture focussed on sustainability. Vince told FIFA TV in 2017:

'We brought all of our missions which are mostly focussed around energy, transport and food.'

It is also really pleasing to note that, in its 2021 Annual Review of Football Finance, accountancy firm Deloitte set the kind of targets that clubs like Forest Green are at the vanguard of:

'What can the football industry do? Football's impact on climate change can be improved through enhanced coordination of organisations educating themselves on the issues and investing resources effectively.'

So, whereas St. Pauli coalesced around a ragtag assortment of laudable and disparate causes, FGR has a much tighter remit of showcasing the philosophy of this major local employer. They also have the ideal catalyst to run these initiatives through the personality of Dale Vince. As a former new age traveller, he would fit right into the ecologically aware ranks of fans at the Millerntor-Stadion. *The Independent*'s Tom Pilston couldn't help but be drawn to his personality:

'I was intrigued. Having met numerous, hugely successful entrepreneurs down the years it's rare to find someone who sticks so firmly to their hippy roots.'

Pilston is right to assume this and is supported by Simon Kuper in his authoritative 2009 book *Soccernomics*:

'Entrepreneurs who dip into football also keep making the same mistakes. They buy clubs promising to run them "like a business" and disappear a few seasons later amid the same public derision as the previous owners.'

We're the perfect blend

What sets people like Vince apart from mere mortals is their restless mental itch to keep improving and never settle for second best. Like James Dyson and the 5,127 iterations of his cyclone method of vacuum cleaning, there is never a resting point. This season, the club have doubled down on their bamboo creation by adding another combination of ingredients to the shirt mix: coffee waste and recycled plastic bottles. This mixture is felt to be more eco-friendly and lighter to wear than the current bamboo mix. Vince explained to the media:

Maybe, just maybe, as Forest Green climb the league ladder and fill in the remaining stars on their shirts, they could link up with their German soulmates and drive forward their joint agendas of tolerance, sustainability and innovation. The world, and especially the football world, would be a much better place for it.

'We think it's lighter than the bamboo, and apparently it breathes better, which is a surprise to me, but there is a performance benefit from minimising plastic because you sweat more and get hotter. But you need that blend because the shirts also need to be super tough.'

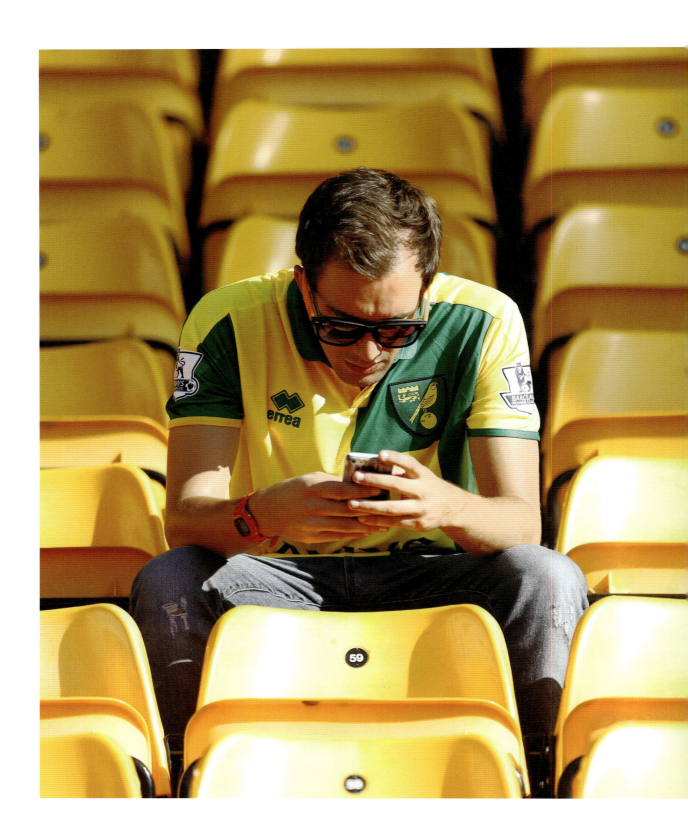

Wears the Money

In my years working in Thai football, I came across plenty of dreamers, schemers and social misfits. Much of the time, a meeting with one or all of them would be arranged with the hidden agenda of fishing for contacts I had accumulated with players, coaches and chairmen. In 2013 a man called Kenny Ager, Sports Revolution Asia's head of strategy, had been pumping me for contacts to get into Thai football's pitchside LED advertising hoarding market.

So an invitation to the Four Points Sheraton in central Bangkok to leverage my friendship with the heir to the Singha Corporation empire Pawin Bhirombhakdi (who had kindly promoted my football website in the stadium LED of his club Bangkok Glass, now known as Pathum United) was offered. What struck me about their slick presentation was how they were way ahead of their competitors. Unfortunately, as Apple has demonstrated regularly, you need to be ahead but not too far in front, or all the unintended consequences of your ideas will come flying directly at you while your competitors are protected from the fallout by your innovators' slipstream.

The key part of their presentation was their development of an app that, when pointed at the shirt's crest, would activate exclusive fan content and offers. It also gave fans access to Footballfancast.com, an egalitarian platform for sharing opinions. But even though Thailand, like much of Asia, was a heavy early adopter of smartphones this was way ahead of the infrastructure to support it. Thai clubs had only just started to engage with fans, and often in an amateurish way, on social media platforms. The leap of faith into an integrated system based on their club shirt seemed – and turned out to be – far too big a leap of faith. Although Footballfancast.com remains a standard gossip and results website, the kit crest app has long gone, but our life of saturated technology seems the right time to bring it back. As I reviewed earlier in the book, the Norwegian side Tromsø and Hashtag United might be the start of a movement that has taken eight years to take hold. Watch this digital space.

We are now generally less sensitive (or savvier) to data mining and with attention fractured fans now seeking new ideas on an increasingly regular

basis, activating our shirt as a portal to engage with our club has strong potential. As Simon Kuper noted in *Soccernomics*, social media is no longer an add-on but a central part of watching games, 'Many of them watch games while bantering with other fans on their mobile phones – the so-called "second screen", though it's rapidly becoming the first screen as it's often more entertaining than the game itself.'

South-east Asia, where a fan will often be wearing a fake kit and watching the game on a pirated Middle Eastern or South African feed, is ripe for monetisation. The key to switching is to personalise the message so that, even if Somchai supports you for free, you can find out all the habits, brands and club sponsors he may buy and, with a nudge through discounts or special offers, activate him to buy more or switch to products he hadn't consumed before. A kit app puts clubs back on the financial front foot to leverage his support indirectly by his purchases, forcing up what your sponsors need to pay for your name. Luckily for Manchester United and Somchai when reading the third page of official sponsors, he can show his support when slurping his next delicious bowl of Thai noodles.

Even if he is wearing a fake shirt, he can be data mined, boxed and delivered to sponsors, just like tens of millions of others. And, as Deloitte's 2021 Annual Review of Football Finance suggested, the technology to make shirts a portal to fan activation is just around the corner. Taking up the momentum started all those years ago, the report published in July 2021 talks about how:

'Diversifying revenue sources, particularly through embracing digital technology, has been a focus of leading European football clubs in recent years.'

Clearly, this makes sense (let's not talk about Zuckerberg's Metaverse please) as technology has seeped into every aspect of our lives. The report also shows the uncertainty we all feel when dealing with such volatile and poorly regulated technology transactions as NFTs and the intangible aspect of the digital world instead of the reassuringly physical and countable process of selling shirts. Here the report falls into marketing word salad when trying to plot a path to effectively monetising the digital space, 'Deloitte help our clients move beyond ad-hoc, siloed, digital initiatives to create a coherent end-to-end transformation that combines emerging technology and human experience-led design.'

Shirts are a window into our personalities, but something tells me that moves are afoot to turn them into portals to NFTs. The report had a whole chapter on them and, possibly more frighteningly, described them as 'novel, tantalisingly lucrative, yet accessible to everyone'.

Maybe the Luddites had a point.

14

A Game Without Shame

Betting's Mutation

There are people in the bookies. They think it's all over. It is now.

Perhaps surprisingly, the first club to have betting shirt sponsorship was Fulham in the 2002/03 season with Betfair (an oxymoron if ever there was one). Also, surprisingly, that deal fizzled out after a year with the Cottagers' board unsure how sponsorship success could be measured effectively. Before gambling there was beer. Shirts try to focus on one vice at a time. Joshua Robinson recalls in *The Club*:

'Spurs had only signed its first jersey sponsorship deal with the brewer Holsten in 1983, becoming one of the last top-flight teams in the league to splash a corporate logo across its famous white shirts.'

Given the stranglehold betting companies now have on the game, the next steps in betting shirt sponsorship were also tentative. 888.com would sponsor Middlesbrough for three years starting in the 2004/05 season.

KIT&**CABOODLE**

Blackburn (then in the Premier League) had Bet24 for 2006/07 and in the same season, Aston Villa had 32Red. But the deal that started betting's exponential profile rise in English football came when Mansion paid Tottenham an annual £14m from the 2008/09 season in a four-year deal. This became the new benchmark and now appears paltry by comparison. The seismic cultural shift from clubs as gatekeepers and sponsors as nervous guests had been turned on its head.

Despite many furtive politicians fruitfully looking away when the harm gambling causes is spotlighted by campaigns like Gambling with Lives, there was a hopeful symmetry on 17 February 2022 when Championship Bristol City severed all ties with the same company. Mansion would be replaced by an overarching sponsorship from local delivery fulfilment business Huboo that not only covered the football club, but also Bristol Bears rugby and the Bristol Flyers basketball team for both the men and women. This is surely a route out of the gambling mire that may not be as lucrative (Bet365 had over £2.1bn in the bank at end of 2020/21 and their CEO Denise Coates could collect £249m that year – still a drop of £172m from the previous year) but something to create pride instead of shame.

As part of the segmentation of the football shirt market, there are even sponsorship agreements for the training kits with Leicester and Manchester City billboarding betting brands during their warm-up and training sessions.

This gives the gambling companies more screen time on a matchday to amplify their ubiquitous ads wrapped around every commercial break. After the interminable pandemic lockdowns, it seems only a matter of time before clubs have betting firms displayed on their pre-match facemasks. Shirt sponsorship has been the vanguard of packaging betting as simply another element of the matchday experience with beers, subscriptions and social media. As Simon Kuper notes, betting may lose the odd skirmish with regulators, but it won the football war a long time ago, 'In fact, sports gambling is now a bigger business than sport itself.'

In her excellent 2021 Channel 4 documentary, *Football's Gambling Addiction*, former politician Ruth Davison described the relationship as 'a parasite that's taking over the host'.

Gambling companies are training so much of their fire on the English games because in countries like France, Germany and Italy stringent regulations limit shirt betting sponsorship. In Spain, a ban on such shirt sponsorships came into effect in 2020. Previously eight of the smaller La Liga clubs were gambling-sponsored. The new rules prevented gambling companies from being allowed to sponsor stadium names or any other aspect associated with the teams. Rules are even harsher in

Australia, where gambling adverts were recently banned during sports events shown before the watershed. Premier League matches also have a history of gambling. According to AFP globally almost £1bn is gambled on each Premier League match and a cumulative global audience of 3.2 billion for all programming watched the action between August 2018 and May 2019, while the BBC's *Match of the Day* draws in an average of four million weekly viewers. These eyeballs are gold mines for betting companies; 95 per cent of TV advertising breaks during the UK live football matches contain at least one gambling advert just to make sure they are constantly trained on their 'service'.

In the UK, tired of waiting for government inaction, campaigns like

The Big Step took a more proactive approach to addressing the social carnage gambling is causing on mobile phones across the land. By November 2021 they had been joined by eight clubs who committed to banning all gambling advertising at their club. Alongside our friends at Forest Green were Luton Town and Tranmere Rovers. These three also supported Fair Game UK and Her Game Too, showing a strong value-driven ethos that gives some hope we can extricate the game from these pernicious forces preying on us at vulnerable moments of emotion. The other teams were non-league and their bravery in refusing a potential gambling lifeline can only be roundly applauded when every penny lost could be an existential act. The weekend of 9 and 10 April 2022

was a case study in why The Big Step needs to be heard when, of the 20 Premier League clubs playing, 18 wore gambling companies on the front of their shirts. The gambling lobby's back-pocket politicians' insistence that advertising does not increase the number of gamblers joining this race to the bottom sounds cruel and purposefully obtuse. Shame on them.

But the fans are fighting back. At the beginning of November 2021's annual Safer Gambling Week, Chance United created an incredibly thought-provoking kit with Michael Louth's take on how design can help raise awareness about gambling. His design was made up of quotes framed by betting slips chronicling the heartbreaking toll that gambling takes on the lives of so many people mixed in with statistics of this senseless waste. The front-of-shirt sponsor was The Big Step. Stitched into the neck was the club's motto of 'a chance for change' and each shirt had the number 13, reminding wearers of their bad luck to be in the thrall of this devastating addiction. All profits from the sales went to Gambling With Lives, a charity supporting those who have lost friends and family members to gambling-related suicide, and the kits sold out, so there is hope to be had. The

organisation shared on 3 March 2022 how 89 per cent of Premier League and EFL clubs have sponsorship on their shirts. Truly frightening.

Club shirts may not be the headline-grabbers among the 47 recommendations of Tracey Crouch's report, but they stand as litmus paper for a report looking to empower and enfranchise fans. There is no clearer place for supporters to see links to local roots like Bournemouth's back-of-shirt sponsorship by local property company DWP or the huge range of clubs adding the Her Game Too logo to their shirts. On the other side of the morality ledger is Watford's sleeve deal with the cryptocurrency 'meme stock', Dogecoin. Not only is their main shirt sponsorship by Curacao-based online sports betting company and crypto casino Stake paid for using cryptocurrency, but their sleeve sponsor for the 2021/22 season was Dogecoin: a creation originally started as a joke currency in 2013 but has gone on to be a favourite of Elon Musk.

Southampton's Sportsbet.io is run through the tiny Caribbean island of Curacao with its two per cent corporate tax rate and invisible touch oversight. Brentford have advertised their focus on the environment and their fans' pockets by extending their kit change cycle which speaks to their priorities and how their shirts can act as a visible manifesto for their ethics while Brighton's sponsors American Express, like Stoke City and Bet365,

have their shirts as one item of the sponsorship menu that also includes stadium naming rights. Only Villa have specific gambling sleeve sponsors as small logos don't convey the message to the countries in Asia where they target circumventing the laws against gambling, but three other clubs in Watford, West Ham and Wolves chose the modern twist on making a bet with crypto and online trading masquerading as 'financial services'. Łukasz Bączek, head of marketing at Intelly, described 2021 as 'a turning point for the cryptocurrency industry' with 17 of the Premier League's 20 clubs connected to one or more commercial deals in this unregulated and highly speculative field. He also highlighted the ethically dubious practice of players marketing them when fans are often under-informed about the 50 per cent that goes to the club and the risk of losing all their stake. Platforms like eToro, Crypto.com, Socios and Sorare have grown profile by making deep and lucrative club connections. Everton, Leeds, Arsenal and Manchester City have signed what are understood to be seven-figure deals with the Socios platform.

Crypto is just the same shit sandwich using a different kind of bread...

Crypto is not new to football, but its exponential profile and growth are. In 2018, investment platform eToro used Bitcoin to pay for a sponsorship deal with seven league teams, and Arsenal signed a cryptocurrency sponsorship deal with CashBet. Southampton's training kit is sponsored by 'educational' Learn Crypto, while digital entertainment company Animoca has partnered with City Football Group to develop blockchain games and collectables for three of the group's teams: Manchester City's men and women, and Melbourne City. Liverpool joined the blockchain collectables startup Sorare. In early February 2022, another stealth move to maximise the dumb funnel of crypto speculators armed only with optimism and greed was forged with Manchester United. Blockchain platform Tezos have stolen a march on their competitors by offering the club an annual £20m just to be on their training kit. The deal partially fills the hole created by the end of the agreement with what now

feels like a quaint old-school business of insurance by Aon. To its acolytes, Tezos lets consumers make more efficient financial transactions that cut out the grasping hands of banks. For distractors, this is yet another delivery system for crypto trading, using Tezos's digital token Tez to gain entry to the Wild West of high volatility and huge price peaks and troughs. There was also, for a fossil like me, the chilling addition that this deal would move from the training kit to leveraging the club's fanbase and history in the 'metaverse'.

But some clubs are starting to reverse engineer a semblance of due diligence. In January 2022 Manchester City ended their partnership with evasive crypto company 3Key Technologies after just two months when a cursory online search of their executives revealed stock photos of unknown people. Better late than never, I suppose.

Bączek's report on shirt sponsorship, released on 23 December 2021, suggested the lower teams are in the Premier League, the more central shirt sponsorship is to their long-term financial sustainability. And they tend to be in a firmer grip from gambling companies. Nine of the 20 clubs had gambling companies on the front of their shirts, contributing £63.25m of the total of £358.75m in the 2021/22 season, one more club than the previous season. In 2019/20 there was huge profile growth for gambling companies, occupying half of the clubs' shirts. Bączek pointed out:

Gambling companies are likely willing to pay more than most non-gambling companies to partner with smaller clubs, while big ones have more options to choose from.

The huge rise in betting logos on shirts is driven by their ability to be far more nimble than traditional businesses and, being such a cash-rich industry, they can seal deals at speed. When Southampton lost their Chinese firm LD Sports' sponsorship just before the 2020 season Sportsbet.io jumped in to fill the shirt gap immediately. Once they gain a foothold they can then infest the whole ecosystem with their pernicious message to the extent that betting logos are placed on physios' shirts over their heart as they race on to attend to a stricken player. They also have a much broader remit than their competitors for 'eyeballs'. They simply need exposure rather than a targeted geographic focus. The camera lens makes a cold evening at St Mary's just another global shop front. They don't even care if the club's fans use their product.

For some, they don't even need to be in English, like all three of Newcastle United's 2021/22 kits. How little it matters that attending fans can see the betting logos and how important that the shirt ad is beamed to a global and increasingly online audience was shown when West Ham brought out two home kits for fans in 2021,one with the betting logo on and one without. The betting company could have kicked up a fuss and demanded a refund, but as long as the broadcasters incentivise gambling by giving it such high prominence both on the kits and around the stadiums, fans can wear what they want as far as the predatory betting behemoths are concerned.

But not all of the online universe funnels us into financial ruin. At the end of 2021, Liverpool found an innovative way to access the world's gamers for merchandising gain by partnering with 'online multiplayer battle royale game' PlayerUnknown's Battlegrounds. Thumb-twizzlers could unlock a limited edition Liverpool kit in-game and be painlessly freed from their money without having to go to the effort of opening a separate website. As depressing as this sounds for a fossil like me, it seems an innovative approach from Liverpool to combine their huge brand appeal with the ability to sell their shirts as rewards instead of purchase decisions. Shirt consumption is moving from an explicit action to purchase to an Amazon wardrobe process where you have to uncouple yourself from the purchase rather than actively seek it.

Pitchside advertising is peppered with Thai, Vietnamese and Mandarin while shirts are often Asia-facing as exercises in 'global reach'. In his coruscating, compelling book *Can We Have Our Football Back?* John Nicholson sets out his manifesto for reclaiming the club shirt for the love of the game, not the gambler's remorse. He argues that the Premier League era (as if 1992 was Year Zero and there was no such thing as a First Division era) has morphed from a socially cohesive fan-driven culture to a 'platforming' environment where fans are paying tourists at a game that is just another carnival of consumerism:

'It wouldn't be fair to lay the problems created by the flourishing online betting industry wholly at the door of the Premier League, but it has become the main platform for driving the growth of some of the most venal, amoral capitalist businesses which will seek to make profit out of anything, no matter how destructive.'[9]

[9] Nicholson, J., *Can We Have Our Football Back?: How the Premier League is Ruining Football and What We Can Do About It,* p124 (Head Publishing, Kindle edition)

Like an Amazon Marketplace for football, the Premier League also offers platform access to 'partners' in return for a cut and the sponsor is saddled with the risk. Whoever you are and whatever you are selling, jump on to our shirts for a fee and you will be admonished by brand association. What marketers call the halo effect. One rather sweet example of this happened in April 2021 when Plymouth Argyle announced to the world in the middle of the Covidiotic two-day European Franchise League that they had just agreed terms with their official turmeric partner. The Turmeric Co will hopefully be more excited than us.

But is it too late to cure the disease without killing the patient? The corrosive cancer cells metastasising on our shirts and through our game have burrowed so deep that gambling paymasters have moved beyond simple market expansion and into nod and a wink in-jokes. When Wayne Rooney's move to Derby County as a player-coach in August 2019 was revealed, it was confirmed that he would be wearing shirt number 32. Why? Derby were already sponsored by 32Red, who had opened their wallets further to cover a large portion of Rooney's salary, using him and his influence to hoover up the last of the gambling laggards. In 2019 Paddy Power pretended to sponsor Huddersfield Town with a garish sash design. The club were used as patsies for part of Paddy Power's social media campaign to create white noise about the event just to ditch it and move on

to the next mark as the season started. Their decision to 'unsponsor' through their Save our Shirt Campaign just made everyone involved in the stunt seem tawdry and desperate. The slave has, according to Nicholson, become the master. Even his own job at Football365 is part-financed by Bet365. Shirts have been the delivery system to infiltrate and modify football's DNA. Now mutated, its chromosomes gravitate to the buzz of constructing complex formulae where goals are a frustrating distraction from an assortment of spot bets.

Gambling has also found ways to mutate further. The doomed Football Index may be referred to as a football betting company now it has gone bust, but that was not how it marketed itself when it was launched. It tried to piggyback the exponential growth of small online investors on platforms like Robinhood and Trading 212 by promoting itself as a 'football stock market'. Picking through the bones of this pseudo-Ponzi scheme trying to hoover up 'dumb money' from fans wanting to leverage their knowledge of the game despite the Gambling Commission warning the company in January 2020 that it was 'an exceptionally dangerous pyramid scheme under the guise of a football stock market' is a depressing process.

This must have come as a shock to QPR and Nottingham Forest who hastily dropped displaying the company's logo on their shirts in March 2021 when news of its collapse came through.

But, with one head removed, the Hydra simply moved on to the next platform. If we couldn't be persuaded to run up huge losses with the Football Index, there was also the largely unregulated world of cryptocurrency to move into. Whatever my 18-year-old son may say, the massive volatility and lack of intrinsic value or oversight is a recipe for financial disaster for those who are not armed with the right kinds of information. On 24 September 2021 Southampton shared how they were 'delighted to put learncrypto.com on their training kit'. Again, this was a disingenuous platform that suggested it was an educational service but was simply another pipeline to mainline hapless fans assuming that the club they loved had done their due diligence. The club chose not to add below the logo the FCA's chilling advice to anyone considering 'investing' their rent money on this highly speculative platform. There is something heartless and heartbreaking about our clubs tapping into the optimism of uncertainty knowing that, with no regulation in place for the fans, they can lose everything but the club will already have banked everything and can simply remove the logo from their shirts as if it had never happened.

'If you invest in cryptoassets, you should be prepared to lose all your money.'

On 10 September 2021, Paris Saint-Germain dived further into the financial Wild West. They signed up Crypto.com as their official crypto partner, but the deal also included the next taxi off the bankruptcy ranks, NFTs. Non-fungible tokens (you wouldn't want your tokens to be funged) are digital units of storage that can capture moments and images but mostly the money of fans. By 25 March Liverpool, depressingly, had joined the New Fleecing Tool with their Heroes Club. The only positive was that it didn't pollute their kits, despite choosing a format in Polygon that generates a huge carbon footprint. At least the women's team were spared what is likely to be a partnership that ends in messy acrimony.

But, even before that fan-rinsing scheme leaves the ranks, we have Socios. It's only a matter of time before betting's latest incarnation is spread across the shirts you see at a ground near you. On 12 December 2021 during Crystal Palace's game against Everton, the Holmesdale Fanatics held up a banner reading 'morally bankrupt parasites. Socios not welcome'. Hijacking the name of Barcelona fan owners is a heartless appropriation tactic, like that of William Hill stealing the feelings towards 'Sweet Caroline' to reel in more punters designed to leverage the love of a club for lucre. To be clear, fans need Socios like a fish needs a bicycle. They may be able to 'engage' with their club by choosing from a preordained list of options for some fatuous poll to decide the colour of the team coach driver's hat, but if the scheme looks like a Ponzi, acts like a Ponzi and smells like a Ponzi, then it's time to crack open the ouija board and summon up the evil spirit of Bernie Madoff.

When talking to the BBC, Socio representative Max Rabinovitch pleaded with reporters Joe Tidy and Edwin Lane that for fans 'the entire point is buy it and hold it'. This could also have come from the cold, dead lips of Madoff. Whatever you do, never sell because, if too many of you do then the scheme falls to pieces. They have learnt from other carpetbaggers preceding them to keep vast tranches of the coins centralised so that, like voting against the Glazers, if a large group tries to sell, they retain ultimate control. Yet again, it is our shirts that are the delivery system for their malignant message by these snake oil salesmen to hypnotise us into abeyance.

Encouraging fans to buy Socios is like asking your local car mechanic to refit a space shuttle. She knows how a combustion engine works and would love to work on a billion-pound piece of kit, but it would be as alien to her as a Socio to a season ticket holder. Before you can buy one you first have to get a cryptocurrency called Chiliz to pay for a token, committing you to two layers of wild fluctuations. If you understand the process, you're not listening properly and the sobering case studies are out there. The NBA's TopShot NFTs allowed fans to own moments of games, an insane concept when you could just watch them for free on YouTube. In less than a year they have dropped by 90 per cent, a classic sign of shady pump and dump figures intoxicating online forums with stories of untold riches before clearing them out and moving on to the next mark. Manchester City didn't help clear up these murky waters in March 2022 when partnering with a company that offers suicidally volatile crypto derivatives illegal in the UK. OKX, based in the Seychelles used a photo of three of City's stars to promote 'the planet's most active crypto derivatives markets'.

The Socio kryptonite is that the best time to invest was yesterday. They perpetuate the myth that, when

rumours of Lionel Messi signing for PSG started circulating, the price would 'go to the moon' then, after he signed the price crashed after they had milked their profits and fans were left trying to catch a falling knife.

When the BBC asked every Premier League club to comment about their relationship with Socios and only Brighton replied (to adamantly deny they will enter this foetid market) it spoke volumes about their sheepish acceptance of new revenue streams that are unregulated and poorly understood by customers. All risk sits with fans and it is disingenuous for them to be compared to trading in foreign currency when cashing in any gains is not anywhere near as simple. There is an elephant in the room here too. If you want to engage with fans meaningfully, then season ticket holders or trust board members are a good place to start. Organisations like Fair Game give fans not only a platform to pursue better oversight of the game, but connections with MPs and high profile figures in sport and academia.

Fans have invested money, loyalty and dogged perseverance. Two out of those three simply don't get Socio intermediaries that extra bonus run through Malta, Estonia and Switzerland.

There is something heartbreaking about Inter Milan's 23-year shirt deal with Pirelli finishing because, in a time of financial hardship, the desperately needed £17m from Socios helped them park their concerns with their paycheque. At least West Ham fans fought back in 2019 and the club cancelled their deal, only for Socios to pop up again with more vigour at Arsenal, Villa, Leeds, Everton and Manchester City.

This financial smoke and mirrors is the symptom, not the disease. It speaks of passion being leveraged: schemes hatched to set fans free from their money due to a lack of independent oversight. Most fans would cross the road to avoid these schemes, but Socios have made their way into club mailing lists to claim false legitimacy. Gambling was mentioned nine times in the Crouch report but there was no mention of NFTs, Socios or cryptocurrency. There is a clear and present danger that needs addressing. If we don't act quickly, another pillar of our game will be kicked away and the lunatics will be given the keys to the asylum.

The harmless obsession with football, whose main by-product was bored partners and pub quiz mastery, has been genetically modified to produce bankrupting financial punishments shadowed by secret shame and, like a GameStop share price, circuitously plunging you towards financial disaster. And now the front of the shirt is not enough. By having an atomised shirt sponsorship hierarchy, betting companies can relentlessly tap into our pre-match excitement and convert it into spending opportunities. Eight gambling companies were Premier League shirt sponsors in 2021,

but only two were on the sleeves and fronts for lower-profile teams (West Bromwich Albion and Burnley) and Villa were only sleeve sponsored by gambling company LT. These companies don't need the platinum sponsorship package and all the costs and commitments associated with it. A top-six club's shirt sponsorship could cost £35m to £50m a season. But for the rest of the teams, the price is generally below £10m and can go as low as £2m annually. The same eyeballs see the logos at a lower entry cost. When a Manchester United player is tussling with a Crystal Palace one, whose shirt the logo is on is irrelevant if the all-seeing camera picks it up. The bigger clubs can hold out for multi-year deals with potential extensions but the betting firms who are in tight competition with each other might find it more strategic to have multiple short-term deals in place spanning just one or two seasons with smaller, and cheaper, clubs to deal with.

The tide seems to be turning with betting's hold over the game. The terrible societal havoc being wreaked has even reached the ears of those in Westminster but, with the bottomless pockets of lobbyists, phrases like 'under consideration' are more likely to lead to highly targeted political donations from gambling companies than any real shift in culture. 'Weighing up the merits' is a calling card for fruitful discussions in expensive restaurants. There will also be plenty of lobbying from the clubs accessing these oceans of

cash. But not all lobbying is undertaken with sticky fingers. Matt Zarb-Cousin is the director of lobbyists Clean Up Gambling, and he lays bare the stark new culture of a slash and burn to fans' hard-earned income not just for now, but in generations to come:

'The evidence shows this sort of advertising is impacting negatively on children who are growing up thinking you have to put on a bet to enjoy sport.'

We must hope that the devil taking the hindmost approach to gambling is at least starting to be challenged. The 'mood music' suggested that a change would come in the autumn of 2021, but that was kicked into the long grass. It feels too late to stop the spiralling lockdown debts of bored and hidden problem gamblers, but there may be a tipping point coming. Worryingly, the point highlighted in much of the reporting is how teams in the top two divisions would take a combined revenue hit of £110m a year if legislation is effectively enacted. The catastrophic financial and societal damage being caused by the rise of poorly regulated gambling seems to have been largely overlooked. Labour MP Carolyn Harris, one of the leaders in the Cross Party Group on Gambling Related Harm, told *The Telegraph* she was confident of the ban being put in place, 'For me, it's about common sense prevailing over greed, because these football clubs have alternative ways to be funded.' Let's hope she's right.

Polling by Survation recently revealed that a third of fans surveyed said they would be put off buying their team's shirt if it included sponsorship from a gambling firm. But for me, that is like an election exit poll. You tell the surveyor what they want to hear but carry on your merry way regardless.

When calmer heads test the logic of every Premier League match needing to generate £9m of TV deal money to break even, losing revenue feels particularly painful. With consistent exponential global growth, any slowing down will seem like gloss flaking off the previously gold-plated Premier League brand and people may start to re-evaluate how much they are willing to pay to ride this gaudy carousel. Never give a consumer time to reflect because, as Warren Buffet so prophetically said, 'Only when the tide goes out do you discover who's been swimming naked.'

The Times Team of The Year for 2021 used a heartbreaking education campaign called Gambling with Lives to illustrate the terrible damage being wreaked daily by the control gambling companies have over our game. Fronted by goalkeeper Lewis Carey, at Bristol City as a youngster before moving into non-league football, the campaign gave a voice to the families bereaved by gambling-related suicides. Lewis has battled with gambling since he signed his first professional contract as an 18-year-old, and he explained:

'As a footballer in recovery from a gambling addiction, I'm excited to be involved in this partnership. With my own experiences of how harmful gambling can be, I feel it is vital that this excellent programme reaches as many young people as possible in the club's community.'

As part of their value-driven approach to the game, Lewes never accept sponsorship from gambling companies. In 2019 they even played with a Gambling With Lives logo on the front of their shirts. Club representatives visited schools to talk to early teen students being groomed by social media for a future life of gambling and rolled the programme out to their youth and local community teams. This is surely a template to lead the fightback against those preying on our children, hiding in plain sight.

15

Only in Thailand

My time in Thai football was a surreal experience and the shirts reflected it. Visiting Buriram United, located in an impoverished region of the northern part of the country, I was stunned to see the size of the crowds and stadium (an exact copy of the King Power).

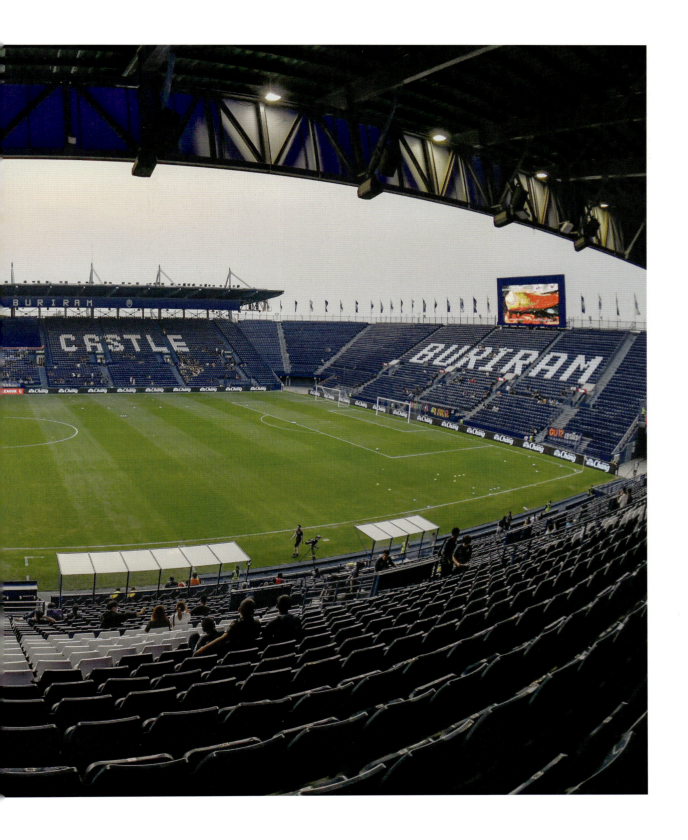

Walking around it, Sven-Göran Eriksson when his Leicester City side visited the kingdom was amazed to see that even the toilets were in the same place as its twin. The other thing that astonished me was that, in this area of farmers toiling in brutally hot conditions often for a subsistence wage, almost everyone was wearing a pristine team shirt. It was only later that I found out that chairman Newin Chidchop had not only handed them out for free, but also paid for fans' food, away travel and medical expenses. Having essentially professional fans is such an alien concept for us here, but when you have shelled out $17m (and this was in 2010) to build your stadium then you need to make sure as many of your 32,600 seats as possible are occupied. Through his business dealings, the self-styled 'King of Buriram' had partnered with Leicester and has continued to make meaningful connections. Not all Thai clubs have fared as well, however.

Atlético Madrid trumpeted their 'strategic alliance' with Muang Thong United in 2010. Atlético CEO Miguel Gil openly explained their need for cash for their new stadium and how they were happy to sleep around to get it. They showered love on Chicago Fire, Shanghai Shenhua and six other 'strategic partners'. This was clearly not a monogamous relationship for one side. So why did the Thai team agree to it? The alliance promised player exchanges, friendly matches and mutual merchandising, but the then Muang Thong coach went off message, suggesting no Atlético player would go his way. *Los Colchoneros* ('the mattress makers') made the bed and

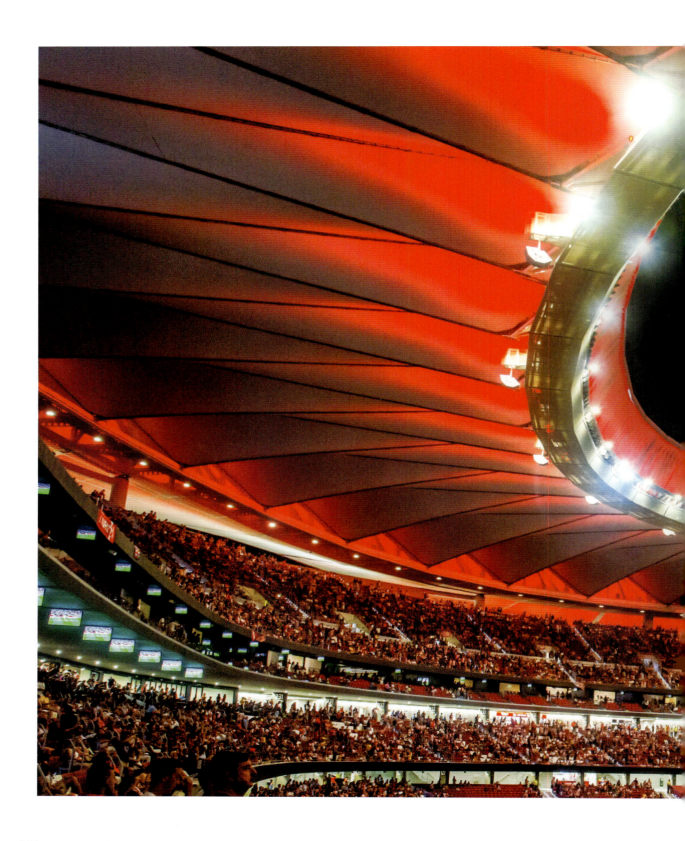

KIT&**CABOODLE**

their lovers were expected to lie in it. Maybe the fact we didn't exchange shirts was ominous.

I look back on that glitzy evening with a mixture of embarrassment and doomed acceptance. The commitment to create a 'strategic alliance' with the Spanish powerhouses that would see both clubs share a range of enticingly unstated activities that remain dormant to this day seems so inevitable on reflection. I can't help looking back on the photo of myself and coach-at-the-time René Desaeyere with the Spanish PR man and wondering if his hands were resting on our backs, or symbolically picking our pockets. The one clear request of the night, stated in startlingly bold terms by Gil, was Atlético's need for cash to finance their new stadium. The Estadio de La Peineta (later renamed the Wanda Metropolitano) cost €250m, but the only tangible result of that unconsummated love-in is how part of it was paid for by the Thais. The towering, extremely affable and startlingly straight-talking Gil made no bones about their web of alliances across the world spanning China, the UAE, Morocco, Mexico, Brazil and Turkey all being revenue streams and, I have to confess, I found his approach refreshingly honest in a football world often showing the integrity of a LinkedIn status update.

A more productive connection for the creaking ex-champions was their informal one with Arsenal, seeing academy players go to north London and the then performance supervisor Steve Morrow flying over here to assess academy teams.

The 'partnership' between BEC Tero and Arsenal was a sobering one. Other than a 2006 kick-around at their London Colney training ground, the Gooners allowed the Thai team to use their kit (forcing the Thais not to sell copies to their fans) and little else of substance. Tero joined other partners in Colorado Rapids and Vietnam's Hoang Anh Gia Lai buried deep in the Arsenal website. This does not a commitment make.

For real commitment, you had to be a Warlords fan. Supporting the Thai side Saraburi is not a glamorous experience. In their 'heyday' the club expected fans to travel around the country from their provincial base 100km north of Bangkok to the unspectacular stadiums of Big Bang Chula or Thai Tobacco Monopoly, and they even expected the shirts off their backs. The match against doomed Nakhon Pathom United in 2014 was prefaced by the kind of preparation that would embarrass a chimp's tea party.

Home team Saraburi couldn't locate a second kit and Nakhon Pathom, a club notorious for being shut down for two years in 2010 when a member of staff threatened a referee with a gun after a promotion play-off game, hadn't brought one. A visit to the local shops came up with nothing – not a surprise in a region proud to be the hub of 'herbal Chinese pork sausage with iodine'. The club managed to fish some socks and shorts out of a kit bag, but it was the unwitting fans who had to hand over their shirts for the greater good of the club.

The Bangkok Casuals League still laughs about the Winking Frog's failure to provide an alternative kit, but this is supposed to be a higher standard of oversight. There is a non-league structure in Thai football called the King's Cup that feeds into a six-league regional setup (skip that if you are a powerful politician) which then moves on to the national system, crowned by the relative glamour of the Thai League 1.

So, a team that can legitimately expect to play at a 36,000-capacity stadium in Buriram the following season forgets to bring a spare kit and, comically, irons on players' names to fans' shirts minutes before kick-off. This being Thailand, both clubs blamed each other and accused their opponents of not communicating. It also says a great deal about Saraburi's merchandising power that their souvenir shop couldn't (or wouldn't) cough up a full set of away kits.

The good news for the shirtless Saraburi supporters was the game finished in a 1-0 victory thanks to their generosity when an automatic two-goal defeat would have been registered if they chose not to strip. The club would go on to be promoted that season and owed a huge debt of gratitude to their topless fans for going over and above the call of duty.

Musical Kits

A metalhead keen to play your next five-a-side in a 'Highway to Hell' shirt or an England fan attracted by a kit where lions are replaced by guitars crowning whispered words of wisdom 'Let it Be'? Then Dan at Rock n Roll Football Shirts is your man. Started in 2019, this passion project based in the north-west melds its work as indie music producers with a love for shirts underscored by their mission statement of:

Love the music
Love the game
Stand out from the crowd

These are the kind of innovative, and values-driven communities that put club megastores to shame. They are arenas of innovation, interaction and evolving networks that spread footballing passion over the upselling of kits designed with planned obsolescence in mind. The England long-sleeved shirt with 'it's all over now' also seems not only a gorgeous creation, but a depressing foreshadowing of England's Qatar World Cup campaign. Luckily, there are some clubs out there that see the importance of merging music and merchandise to pay forward kindness.

Known as the Bundesliga's 'Carnival Club', FSV Mainz 05 place the Mainzer Fastnacht carnival at their heart, and in January 2022 it was part of the kit. This is no ordinary carnival either. It is a celebration of political and literary humour. Think St. Pauli but with punchlines. After every Mainz goal scored at a home match, the 'Narrhalla March', a famous German carnival tune, is played and the club have decided to go all in on their support for this cultural keystone in the club and community calendar. Post-Christmas hangover January may have been a little early to unleash this gaudy coloured kit, but it certainly got attention. To celebrate surviving another year in the top Bundesliga for the 12th rather unstoried time the club released what their marketing spin optimistically described as, 'the Narrhalla March in fabric form'. Although it is rather a Marmite design, the fans will be used to the colour scheme, if not its latest interpretation. The quietest part of the shirt is the plain white back, and for €85 your eyes and wallet will certainly need some respite by the time you get to it. Having said that, if you wanted to buy a Bayern shirt, you would have to shell out €140 for an 'authentic' (as opposed to a fake?) away shirt and your Mainz purchase goes to support local music groups. As their website shares:

'As this year's jersey features the score for the Narrhalla March, five euros per shirt sold will go to orchestras and music clubs in the region, whose work for the conservation and support of the musical side of our carnival traditions is indispensable.'

Seemingly inspired by the much-envied 50 plus one ownership model for German clubs, there seems a more open desire for them to use their shirts as statements of ethical intent. For their 5 February 2022 game against Frankfurt, Stuttgart played in a shirt supporting their anti-discrimination campaign and marked the liberation of Auschwitz using the central phrase 'Jeder Mensch zählt – Egal auf welchem Platz!' This translates to 'Everyone counts – No matter on what pitch!'

Unfortunately they were to lose 3-2, but a higher message being shared throws our gambling-saturated shirts here in England into the sharpest of

relief. Dutch Eredivisie club RKC Waalwijk also released a vibrant carnival shirt to celebrate their Schoenlappersslaan in February 2022 which was originally only available to active season ticket holders: a great way to make those who commit to the club's future feel valued. The match-worn shirts were then sold with the club donating the funds to humanitarian charities supporting people displaced by the Russian invasion of Ukraine.

KIT&CABOODLE

A football shirt is, thankfully, not only a vehicle to drive more sales, bets and subscriptions. It can also be a platform to promote a musician's love for their club. In May 2021 singer Ed Sheeran announced the sponsorship of his beloved Ipswich Town's men's and women's shirts for the next season. The shirt promoted his album and world tour with an enigmatic logo – not that he needed it.

Sheeran is a boyhood fan of Ipswich, a club high on history but low on recent success (they last played in the Premier League in 2002). Coupled with the spring 2021 takeover by American businessman Brett Johnson, the shirts were a sign of new optimism at Portman Road for a foreign owner saying all the right things and a local boy made good starting a positive momentum that many football romantics were hoping would help them return to the Championship after dropping to League One in 2019.

In the same season, another singer-songwriter, Jake Bugg, continued to be the shirt sponsor of boyhood club Notts County's away shirt. He echoed the feelings of any fans who passionately support their local team when he shared with Notts County's media team:

'It's a surreal but brilliant feeling, especially when we win a big game and the players are all celebrating with your name on the shirt.'

Musical kits don't just hope to be part of the club's future success; they can also be a stylish statement about the club's culture. Already in possession of a crest that was voted by *FourFourTwo* in

its 2021 poll as the second most stylish in world football behind 1860 Munich, Ajax wore a stunning third kit paying tribute to Bob Marley's 'Three Little Birds' song for the 2021/22 season. The song has become their unofficial anthem at the Johan Cruyff Arena and it got me thinking about other kits inspired by songs and singers. Sadly, the killjoys at UEFA would ban the design during Champions League games for taking up valuable space that could help flog cryptocurrency or alcohol, but that just made it even more cherished by collectors.

And collectors often have a huge commitment to pursue their next find. In February 2022 the highly respected Football Shirt Collective wrote a telling piece about why the process of seeking out just one more design for the collection can be so addictive. The writer Phil Delves kindly gave permission to share his blog:

'Let's face it, in a few years' time we might need to form some sort of "collectors anonymous". The football shirt collecting scene has exploded in a big way over the past couple of years, and with every new collector we have one more person potentially wandering dangerously close towards an addiction to polyester.Though I'm largely joking, addiction to buying football shirts is very much a thing, and today in Collectors Club I want to touch on the topic of addiction. Why are we so addicted to buying shirts, and what can we do if we feel like we're losing control?

Why is shirt collecting so addictive?

'Shirt collecting is addictive on a scientific level. Many of you will be familiar with dopamine, the neurotransmitter which our brains send out on a regular basis. When we purchase something we get what's often referred to as a dopamine rush; a surge of chemical messages in anticipation of what's due to arrive through our letterbox. This rush can be a great source of excitement, but that "high" we get can be as much of a blessing as a curse. If we're not careful, we can find ourselves chasing that rush by buying something just for the sake of buying something. Sometimes the shirt we're buying becomes secondary to the fact we've just bought anything at all, and if we're not careful our interest can morph into an addiction (we'll talk at the end of this piece about how to curb a growing addiction).

A never-ending road

With a lot of collecting hobbies, there's a definitive end point. If you start a Panini album for a particular tournament, there are X number of stickers you need to collect before you can call it a day, until the next tournament of course. For football shirts though, it's a little more complicated. In theory there is a number for all the football shirts that have ever been made, but in practice that number is virtually impossible to nail down. With so many shirts and variations of shirts around the world, even the biggest collectors will just be scratching the surface of what is possible to collect.

This could be seen as a negative; a frustrating fact which makes the whole activity of collecting seem somewhat pointless. I'd look at it the other way though and say that the never-ending nature of football shirt collecting makes it exciting. There is always something new to discover, something new to add. We'll never exhaust the well because it is so deep. Of course, to help combat this you can look to collect particular sets as a collector, say all the home shirts from the 1992 Premier League season, or every Parma shirt that's ever been made. These sorts of goals can be invaluable in giving focus and providing some sort of structure within the immense possibilities.

KIT&**CABOODLE**

The nostalgia of football shirts

I observed a clear trend when the pandemic began. When everyone was having to stay at home, all sorts of people came out of the woodwork to enter the football shirt community. It was a joy to behold. Many people who had always had a fondness for kits were amazed to see that there were hundreds of us already talking about them online. When people were stuck at home, they went up to their attic to dig out that box of shirts from the 90s, they hunted eBay to try and recapture a lost kit love from their childhood.

Retro shirt collection

One of the reasons football shirts are so enticing is because they hold so many memories. Whether from a game we attended or of a player we used to love watching, each shirt can conjure up so much emotion. This draw undoubtedly

hooked many people a couple of years ago, and it has been a key reason for starting a collection for many more years before that. It's funny to think that they'll be kids growing up today who'll one day reminisce about the shirts of the 2020s. This cycle will continue and shirts will be there to tell the story each step of the way.

How do you curb an addiction to shirts?

Let's finish with a serious question, how do you curb an addiction to buying football shirts? Though it might sound silly, a hobby of buying shirts can, if left unchecked, spiral out of control. I appreciate this might seem strange coming from a site that is centred around football shirts and buying shirts, but we owe it to everyone to encourage wise spending and healthy buying habits.

The first and often most difficult step is a frank, honest look at exactly what you're spending. It's easy to fall into habits of buying every shirt we see, without any consideration for how much the shirt actually is, but take a step back and see what your typical monthly outgoings are. Once you have a rough figure, you can then weigh this against what money is coming in every month. We'll cover budgeting in more detail in a later Collectors Club, but hopefully this is enough of a nudge to take action in this area.

Football shirt addiction

'Once we know what sort of budget you're working with, consider freeing up cash by parting with shirts you already own, rather than always buying new shirts. The next, new thing is often most attractive, but if you have several shirts sitting in a wardrobe which you've never worn you might be better off selling those shirts to fund new purchases. Many collectors like to keep hold of every purchase they make, but taking a more "fluid" approach to your growing haul can reap huge benefits when it comes to being able to afford shirts.

Phil Delves, Football Shirt Collective

'Though lots of people joke about keeping their spending habits a secret from their friends or significant others, one of the best ways you can curb an addiction to spending is to hold yourself accountable with someone else. Whether a fellow collector or someone who has no interest in buying shirts, being open about that mystery package on the doorstep can help you to self-evaluate whether a purchase is really necessary in the first place. This doesn't mean you need to provide weekly spreadsheets with all your incoming and outgoing purchases, but a simple text or conversation about what you're thinking of buying can help you avoid impulse purchases which you'll regret later.

'Finally, if you feel out of control when it comes to spending you might want to consider just taking a break from the "game". Collecting is often a long-term pursuit, but during that pursuit a break can be the best thing for your enjoyment and mental health. Consider unfollowing social media accounts who push deals, or even coming off social media altogether for a time. Use the opportunity to reflect, re-energise, and enjoy the shirts you already have. Hopefully some of the things I've said in this section have been helpful if you are looking to slow down. If you still need support, can I point you in the direction of CALM (Campaign Against Living Miserably), a wonderful charity who we've worked with here at FSC. Help is out there.'

To find out more about Football Shirt Collective's great work, follow them on @thefootballsc where you'll be joining over 20,000 others pursuing their dream in polyester.

Dublin's completely fan-owned Bohemian Football Club returned to the Marley theme for their 2022 away shirt which, in agreement with the Marley family (Bohs had tried to release an away kit also featuring an image of Marley on the front in 2018 but had to pull it after the Marley estate objected) created a cool collaboration that donates ten per cent of its profits to buy musical instruments and football equipment for people in asylum centres across Ireland. Featuring red, yellow and green details on the front, neck and sleeve trims, an embroidered hem tag of the original concert ticket – celebrating Marley's final outdoor gig at the club's Dalymount Park Stadium on 6 July 1980, remembered as 'An Afternoon in the Park' – on the lower front. A smiling image of Marley is front and centre. This is a design and cause that the football-mad king of reggae would have been proud to support. I also love the added flourish on the shirt back of the embroidered phrase 'Dublin's Originals'. Here, and below, they show who they are in the very best of ways.

In 2021, Bohemians were sponsored by Fontaines D.C., the 'post-punk indie rock' band who were nominated for a Grammy the same year for their album *A Hero's Death*. Not only is their sponsorship of Bohemians' away kit helping raise the team's profile, but 15 per cent of the sales go to support the homeless charity Focus Ireland. Drummer Tom Coll explained to *NME* in March 2021 why the culture of the club was so important in their decision:

'Bohs are an organisation that really care about the community. Having a Dublin football team having "Refugees Welcome" be the biggest thing on their shirt, that's amazing. Politically, in Ireland, we don't like to align ourselves with any party or anything like that, because … I don't know, I feel like they're all shit, man.

'But having a social conscience, when it comes to the setting and the city that you're in, that's really important to us. So that's why we got on so well with Dan and everyone at Bohs because they all think like that and probably to a more intense degree than we do.

'A football club and music and a band can give people a sense of place and you want to have pride in your place.'

This is a wonderfully worthy culture of using the shirt to promote tolerance and kindness over commerce and greed. But there are also fantastically eccentric examples of bands sponsoring shirts. Greenbank FC under-tens B team in 2006 were probably surprised to have their new shirt sponsor as Motörhead. They walked out to the band's iconic anthem 'Ace of Spades'. This must have made some impression on sleepy Sunday morning sideline parents expecting a local timber merchant or greengrocer to show their roots.

Judging by the lifestyles and musical content of the heavy metal bands, it is surprising they were welcomed with open arms. Another 18-certificate band to sponsor a youth team were The Prodigy who sponsored the Eastleigh Reds under-13s in 2012. The trend was started way back in the big-haired 1990s with Wet Wet Wet shirt-sponsoring their hometown club Clydebank FC.

There is plenty of ego in having your name or band on a club's shirt, but there is also something that feels so innocent about it, like the original sponsors of local clubs by local firms, celebrity fan sponsorship over monolithic international companies offshored in the Cayman Islands. It speaks to a club culture welcoming less money than a foreign-based betting behemoth in return for a throwback feeling of community. It also helps to define the chasm between the Premier League and the rest of the 'football pyramid' perpetuating the lie that is 'trickle-down economics'.

Rather than wait for crumbs from the rich club tables, these sponsors are creating their own culture of throwback support designed to help and not leverage. At the top of the tree, clubs squeeze out the last sponsorship opportunity – for example, Tottenham's official paint supplier Dulux – which gets hoovered up by agent fees and unsustainable player wages. By the end of the 2020/21 season, four Premier league clubs were paying out over £300m a year to players, topped by Manchester City at £355m. Even Spurs shelled out £205m.

As podcast host Kieran Maguire described it in a tweet on 14 May 2021, 'When the Premier League started the average UK annual salary was £15,548. By 2019 it had increased to £30,420. If salaries had kept pace with the rise in wages in football it would be £437,084.'

But for those below the golden top tables, shorn of luxuries like an official noodle partner, the tail doesn't need to wag the dog. In return, the shirts can speak of bands who know they won't get a return on this investment but can show their allegiance and approval of how their club is run in a sustainable, transparent and inclusive way.

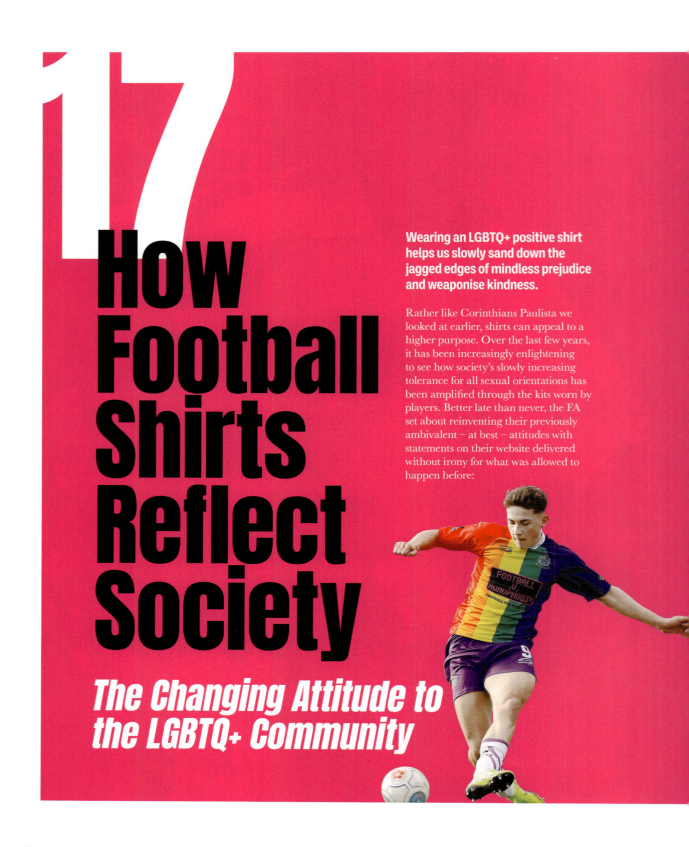

17

How Football Shirts Reflect Society

The Changing Attitude to the LGBTQ+ Community

Wearing an LGBTQ+ positive shirt helps us slowly sand down the jagged edges of mindless prejudice and weaponise kindness.

Rather like Corinthians Paulista we looked at earlier, shirts can appeal to a higher purpose. Over the last few years, it has been increasingly enlightening to see how society's slowly increasing tolerance for all sexual orientations has been amplified through the kits worn by players. Better late than never, the FA set about reinventing their previously ambivalent – at best – attitudes with statements on their website delivered without irony for what was allowed to happen before:

'The FA is uniquely placed to tackle unacceptable and discriminatory behaviour in football. Why? Because as the guardian of the game in this country, The FA will continue to work tirelessly to ensure the game exists for EVERYONE. To work towards a more LGBT inclusive game we will:

- Promote a positive, inclusive image and reputation for the game, its participants and supporters

- Work with LGBT community and football stakeholders to identify boundaries to LGBT participation and work collaboratively and collectively to address them and preserve player and participant welfare

- Support professional clubs and our County FA network in developing good practice around LGBT inclusion and engagement

- Amend the Laws of the Game to outlaw homophobic, bi-phobic and transphobic language and behaviour

- Encourage and support current and future generations of participants from all communities to join the football family, whether as players, match officials, supporters, coaches or administrators/volunteers'

Returning to our friends at St. Pauli, they started this century with one of world football's more enlightened appointments. Cornelius 'Corny' Littmann replaced Reenald Koch as club president in 2003 after receiving 78 per cent in a vote at a general assembly. He was to be the first openly homosexual president of a German football club. While his reign was to be controversial with sections of the fanbase (who he referred to derogatorily as 'Social Romantics') with a stronger focus on sporting and commercial success over and above community engagement, it was refreshing to see him criticised for his decisions over his orientation.

Before the rainbow laces days and captains' armbands supporting the LGBTQ+ community, football was often driven down to the lowest common denominator of neanderthal homophobic imbecility: occasionally with horrific consequences.

'You have to understand that footballers are very narrow-minded people. When you put yourself in the firing line, you are open to attack.'

Justin Fashanu

It's May 1998. In a rundown Shoreditch lock-up hangs the lifeless body of a man paying the ultimate price for society's attitude to homosexuality. He also happened to be the first black player to be sold for £1m and the winner of 11 England under-21 caps.

Justin Fashanu was the victim of a culture that revelled in macho posturing and lived by a don't ask don't tell hypocrisy that had previously forced hordes of gay men to live a bitter lie. Via agent Eric Hall, Fashanu decided to come out as gay in 1990 with a huge splash in *The Sun* peppered with a wide range of lurid and mostly false claims of high-profile assignations with MPs and celebrities. This is the default setting for tabloid 'revelations' nowadays but then, breaking football's taboo was the death knell for his career. He related to *Gay Times* the following year how the article had inflicted 'heavy damage' on his football career. Although fully fit, no club offered him a full-time contract after the story first appeared and let's remember that he was 29 at the time so reaching the peak of his footballing powers. His career took a depressingly downward spiral from 1990 at West Ham via Southall, Torquay and Leatherhead. Fashanu knew he was paying a heavy price for the homophobic pervading culture. As he lamented in that interview:

'You have to understand that footballers are very narrow-minded people. When you put yourself in the firing line, you are open to attack.'

More than two decades after Fashanu was found dead, Australian A League player Josh Cavallo took the step of openly sharing his status as a footballer who was also gay. He is thought to be the only current top-flight footballer to have done this, two years after former Newcastle Jets player Andy Brennan became Australia's first professional male footballer to come out as gay while still playing the game. But now, rather than sensational and mostly false tabloid headlines, it was his club, Adelaide United, who were the platform used. In an article called 'Josh's Truth', his club proudly offered him the chance to speak for many footballers who remain silent about their sexuality:

'Being a gay closeted footballer, I've had to learn to mask my feelings in order to fit the mould of a professional footballer. Growing up being gay and playing football were just two worlds that hadn't crossed paths before. I've lived my life assuming that this was a topic never to be spoken about.'

Although still with a long way to go, football's current culture is clearly far more accepting of differences. But the journey to respect continued to be challenging for Cavallo and others considering sharing their true orientation. He told journalists how he had 'no words' to describe the foetid homophobic abuse he received when his Adelaide United played Melbourne Victory on 8 January when coming on as a second-half substitute.

'It's been such a long time of lying and I've just processed and processed every day of just about how I want to do it, when I want to do it and I think now it's just the right time to do it. You know I feel like I'm ready to tell people about my story.'

Jake Daniels, May 2022

For three decades no current players in the top four levels of English football had come out as gay until Jake Daniels made a decision that we can only hope will, in future, fade into irrelevance as we watch football irrespective of gender, orientation or (in the case of Oldham Athletic) playing ability.

More astonishing than challenging a dressing room environment of often toxic masculinity's taboo first breached by Fashanu in 1990 is the fact that, when the Blackpool forward decided to be honest about his orientation, he was only 17 years old. The calm, mature and heartfelt way he shared his story would be remarkable about any subject. Gary Neville was as stunned and awestruck as us all when talking about the video on *Monday Night Football* 20 minutes after Jake shared it. He commented:

'I was incredibly proud just to see a 17-year-old be able to actually do an interview with that level of quality that our players you know probably wouldn't be able to interview ourselves like that until probably our mid 20s, late 20s.'

He went on to describe how it was, 'a day of great importance for obviously Jake and his family but also I think for English football and it'll go down in history. It's a big, big moment.'

High profile Premier League players like Harry Kane, Eric Dier and Ben Mee showed their support for Jake, an allyship sadly lacking for Fashanu when his news and often divisive personality made potential high-profile mentors take one step back. But, yet again, it was shirts that helped tell the story of kinship created by this honourable young man. For their match against Tottenham (let's not dwell on the score) on 22 May 2022, Norwich City warmed up wearing black t-shirts with the words 'game changer' written in LQBTQ+ rainbow colours combined with 'Jake Daniels. Norwich City are with you.'

Clearly, especially in social media's cesspit, there will be moronic pushback and the messages that shirts share can also flush out people within the game holding narrow-minded views. PSG's Idrissa Gueye allegedly refused to play in a recent game because of the club's rainbow flag on the shirt. Interestingly, he has had less of a problem playing for a club with lucrative multi-year connections with Unibet advertised on his sleeve all season or the strengthening ties with the highly divisive Socios.com.

Our friends at St. Pauli have consistently promoted acceptance of LGBTQ+ fans and the rainbow coloured skull and crossbones in their 2015/16 kit showed how you can be a rebel and promote acceptance without mutual exclusivity. In the same season, Spain's Rayo Vallecano showed their support by redesigning their away kit from having a red sash to a rainbow design. For every shirt sold, €5 would be shared among seven causes that fought against discrimination. This was an impressively mature stance to take, showing that LGBTQ+ rights are part of an inclusion philosophy shared with an alliance of other groups that can draw strength through community, empathy and solidarity.

Newport County, like my Exeter City, are a fan-owned club and they saw the importance of using club shirts as a canvas to paint the picture of equality, diversity and inclusion. In late February 2022 they created a campaign known as My County, My Shirt. The rich range was celebrated through a portrait exhibition of County fans in club shirts. Exiles Together commissioned photographer Kamila Jarczak to produce a collection of portraits taken at Rodney Parade and Newport landmarks followed by an exhibition of the stadium and in matchday programmes.

Stuart Goodwin described the Rayo Vallecano shirt in *The Guardian*, 'The red stripe is for those tackling cancer, orange is for those fighting for the integration of disabled people, yellow is for "those who have lost hope", green is for people striving to protect the environment, blue is for those fighting against child abuse, while pink is for the victims of domestic violence. The rainbow of colours as a whole relates to a seventh cause, those from LGBTQ+ backgrounds facing struggles against discrimination.'

Rayo's umbrella of causes was reflected by Brasileirão club Vasco Da Gama's away shirt released in June 2021. Their usually monochrome sash was transformed into a graduated rainbow marking that month's annual Pride celebrations. The '*Respeito e Diversidade*' amplified Gama's home city of Rio de Janeiro and their proud history of supporting the LGBTQ+ community. Their Copacabana beach even hosted the country's first-ever Pride parade in June 1995. To bring the month to a close, Vasco wore the jersey for their home game against Brusque. After his 63rd-minute goal, Argentine striker Germán Cano ran to the rainbow corner flag and waved it triumphantly as he was mobbed by his team-mates. This felt like an energising and transformational moment in the often macho world of Brazilian football. Vasco's eventual 2-1 win would also send out a message of tolerance and inclusion for a community often marginalised and demonised in the world of Brazilian football.

Pink was also used by Scottish Championship strugglers Queen of the South to highlight the blight of violence against women. Their away kit supported the White Ribbon campaign, something thrown into sharp relief when they played Raith Rovers on 1 February 2022 amid the fallout from Raith's short-lived decision to sign convicted sex offender David Goodwillie.

Two days after Valentine's Day in 2019, National League side Altrincham made a bold statement of their support by designing their whole kit based on the LGBTQ+ Pride flag. Based in Greater Manchester, an area famous for its support of the LGBTQ+ community, Altrincham also scored a tremendous global marketing hit with their confident design and front-foot approach to supporting the Football v Homophobia movement.

Kits are an excellent calling card to start conversations on inclusion, but there is also a more meaningful change that provides a platform for players and fans of the LGBTQ+ footballing scene. Charlton Athletic were the first British club to take the step in 2017 when they signed off on the Charlton Athletic Community Trust. Rather than being a purely LGBTQ+ setup, player-manager Gary Ginnaw explained to Sky Sports's Jon Holmes:

'Two-thirds of the team are straight, one-third are gay and there are no issues whatsoever.'

Four years after the Addicks' bold initiative, I caught up with Zaki Dogliani, Charlton's Community Trust marketing and communications manager, to hear about how it had evolved.

He explained, 'Yes, it was August 2017 when the affiliation first happened. I'd joined the Charlton Community Trust that June so it was one of the first pieces of communication I remember working on. I was made aware that there was an existing team which I believe used to be called Bexley Invicta and that they had a relationship with our equality, diversity and inclusion department which was also fairly modern; ahead of its time in a sense. I believe we were the first community trust to have a dedicated strand so they had some kind of relationship before where we informally supported their matches and they approached us asking if we wanted to go one step further and that's what happened.

'So with the support of the club, we decided to formally affiliate Invictus so they would be fully renamed, rebranded to become Charlton Community Trust Invictus. They had a big launch event in August 2017 at The Valley for them to form the club, including the chief executive.

'Our EDI work has been going for a long time, dating back to the early '90s with some support from the PFA but it's only been relatively recent in terms of the last ten years or so or even less than that when there has been lots happening around LGBTQI+ issues. We now do an annual tournament which is the Charlton v Homophobia tournament at The Valley every summer which Invictus are obviously a part of. In 2018 Invictus and ourselves at the Community Trust and lots of students from the uni took part in the Pride Parade which was fantastic. We also work quite closely with Proud Valiant, which is the official supporters' group. They've had great support from the football club as well with open training sessions. I remember going to watch a training session that the then-manager Carl Robertson did with Lee Bowyer. They use our facilities every week and have weekly training at the club's training ground. They are very much part of the Charlton family. More importantly,

KIT&CABOODLE

though, the people involved in it have a safe place to play football.

'There's so much more to do: it's great to have that team but you always need to raise more awareness. In all stadia in the Football League, there is still homophobic chanting and abuse which even though we've done EDI work in the community for decades we haven't eradicated it.'

One swallow may not make a summer, but a supportive community of like-minded football fans and players gives a platform to show the revolutionary, iconoclastic power inherent in being simply decent and open-minded. The Gay Football Supporters Network shows plenty of that St. Pauli spirit with a mission statement that, after all the abuse they have suffered over the years, could be understandably caustic and exclusive. Instead, they rise above the haters:

'The GFSN league is the world's only national league which is aimed at the LGB&T community and is open to all, regardless of age, race, nationality, religion, gender or sexuality.'

Hamburg, despite being St. Pauli's nemesis, wore a special edition football shirt in their 1-1 draw against Karlsruher on 29 April 2021, to mark the tenth anniversary of the club's LGBTQ+ fan club, Volksparkjunxx. The centrepiece of the shirt is the Volksparkjunxx lettering on the front of the jersey, with the rainbow X representing the Roman numeral for ten. The main sponsor, Orthomol, allowed the fan club's name to take the space usually reserved for its logo. The shirts were part of a limited edition of 1,887 (representing the year Hamburg were founded) and were another step in the process of normalising all support irrespective of race, religion or orientation. This was also a strategy used by Swedish second-tier club AIK Fotboll in February 2022. Their elegantly designed royal blue shirt had only 131 copies available to celebrate 131 years of the club and all proceeds went to Stadium Sports Camp, a non-profit organisation providing young people with access to sport.

Like Black History Month, it must feel quaintly patronising to have time set aside for a profile rather than a daily conversation between people with a rainbow of orientations, but at least it serves to draw a line and develop into an integrated and natural acceptance of differences. Five years ago, LA Galaxy unveiled their pre-match shirt to celebrate their fourth annual Pride Night Game, played each June. Although it was largely welcomed by fans, accusations of 'virtue signalling' and fans pushing back with 'I'm waiting for hetero pride month' showed how much further there was to go.

In 2019 there was another important step into creating a more nuanced discussion about prejudice when Scotland's Partick Thistle launched their subtle support of LGBTQ+ as part of their third kit by using rainbow coloured piping to frame the white shirt. Talking to the BBC, chief executive Gerry Britton showed how the focus had now moved on from sexual orientation to a wider acceptance of differences within a community of respect. The kind of comments that would have a rabid Fox News presenter sputtering into their grits, 'Partick Thistle is one club open to all, we will not accept discrimination in any form and I sincerely hope that this shows that. Football can be such a wonderful universal language that can help bridge all sorts of divides, both large and small. As a club, if we can use this sport that we all love to make all of our supporters feel welcome, even if that is through something as simple as a band of colour on a shirt, then it's a simple decision.'

Three years later, the integration of LGBTQ+ into more adult conversations moved to another level with Stonewall FC's kit collaboration with Adidas. The stylish design shows how the discussion about inclusion and acceptance had matured and taken hold. Subtle design features and sleeve logos supporting Kick It Out and a small rainbow inclusion flag shows confidence, tolerance and collegiality with anyone facing down prejudice.

Football has for too long been one of the last bastions of dark 'banter' and testosterone-fuelled exclusion for any groups seen as deviating from 'the norm'. But shirts have helped herald a new culture of not only accepting differences but learning through profile, celebration and increasing tolerance that every person wearing a shirt has plenty to teach and even more to learn.

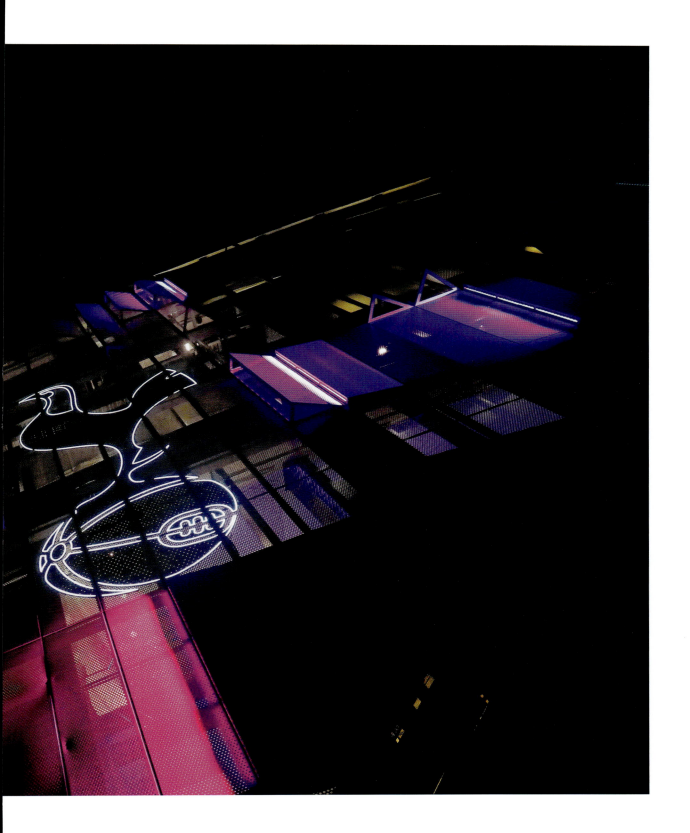

18

'Oh, my eyes!'

What Kit Crimes Say About Football Culture

Brothers Daley and Lewis Jones have an unusual – and expensive – annual Christmas challenge. Each year they source the most car crash kits to swap as a kind of internecine war of mutually assured fashion destruction.

Replacing their previous yuletide default of shopping vouchers, the new approach has sparked a fierce competitive edge in them to find the bottom of the kit design barrel and start scraping. But the competition doesn't stop there. As the BBC related:

'Each year the brothers score each other on three criteria: How obscure the team is, how weird the sponsors are and how "physically grotesque" the shirt is. The winner receives a free round of drinks.'

So far, the holy grail of kit crimes remains a shellfish. Yes, shellfish, inspired abomination from Spanish third-tier team Loja CD. The warning signs for any fan that their designer is a sandwich short of a picnic comes with the club crest that looks like a row of paracetamols crowning three half-eaten battered frankfurters. As a logo, it has the majesty and heft of popcorn.

The competition was at risk of running aground with a dreadful dead heat. This time it is back to Spain with the broccoli tribute design of fellow third-tier strugglers Lorca CF. But why do clubs and fans do this to themselves? They are accelerating

KIT&**CABOODLE**

the cycle of planned obsolescence. In our world of short attention spans and passion for fast fashion, kits can now be ephemerally expensive conversation starters before being shelved and forgotten. This was something Dortmund jumped on in February 2022. The visit of Glasgow Rangers in the Europa League was the club's 1,000th home game, so the cup shirts were given a free added badge featuring the date, 17 February. They also gave a 20 per cent discount which, considering their 4-2 mauling by the Scottish champions, suggests they were about to experience some unplanned obsolescence for the second-tier European competition that they were soon to exit after the second leg at Ibrox.

Pre Premier League, the mother of all fashion faux pas was Coventry City's chocolate confection, unveiled to an unsuspecting public in 1978, 14 years before the Premier League was launched. In many ways, Coventry's approach was an outlier of contemporary thinking but a preface to the Premier League (and chocolate ginger nuts).

They were also the first club to have an all-seater stadium, completing Highfield Road's upgrade 11 years before the Premier League kicked off and, under the direction of Jimmy Hill, adopted an innovative attitude in a football culture often devoid of development. Hill also instigated the first full-colour matchday programmes, and was one of the first to push for a club song, and pre-match entertainment. His asinine *Match of the Day* contributions such as 'It is a cup final and the one who wins it goes through' are easy to mock in a Neville/Carragher world but he was at the vanguard of so many other innovations that were often ridiculed at the time and gave the 1980s glimpses into a '90s football environment. He lifted a ban on media interviews, introduced the first electronic scoreboard and made Coventry the first club to show a live match via CCTV on giant screens. He changed Coventry's colours from white to 'sky blue' in an astute piece of marketing for a club based in a city where 'sky grey' would be a better fit.

Football culture was starting to come out of the monochrome, brutal experiences of the 1970s where going to matches was often a joyless, uncomfortable and outright dangerous decision to make. And this multicolour dawn was being reflected in club kits. The newfound confidence was also underpinned by the sweeping away of terracing. The Taylor Report was published in January 1990, the year after Hillsborough's shocking scenes. One of the key recommendations by the Lord Chief Justice was the removal of perimeter fencing, the creation of all-seater stadiums and far more focus on safety, respectful policing and access to modern, purpose-built facilities.

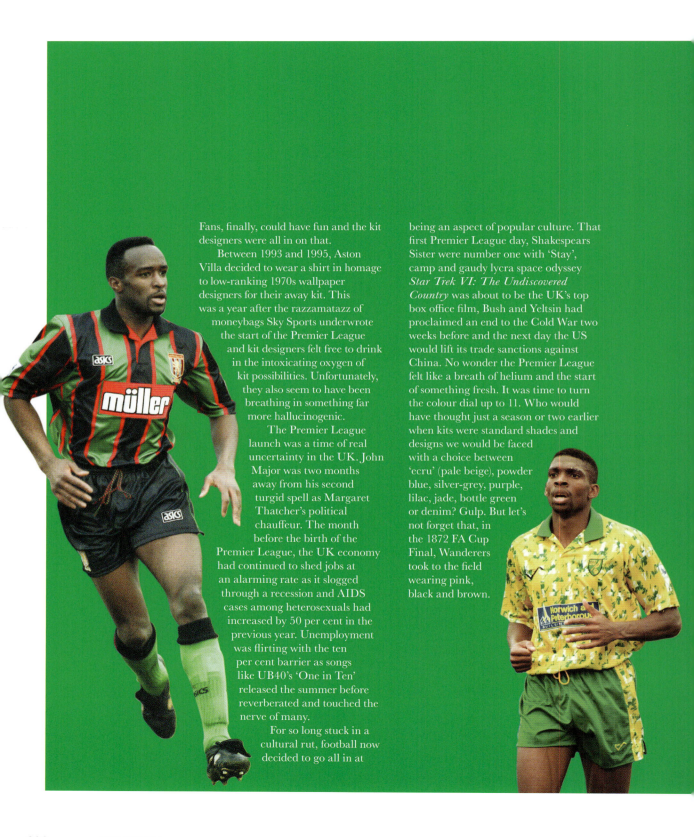

Fans, finally, could have fun and the kit designers were all in on that.

Between 1993 and 1995, Aston Villa decided to wear a shirt in homage to low-ranking 1970s wallpaper designers for their away kit. This was a year after the razzamatazz of moneybags Sky Sports underwrote the start of the Premier League and kit designers felt free to drink in the intoxicating oxygen of kit possibilities. Unfortunately, they also seem to have been breathing in something far more hallucinogenic.

The Premier League launch was a time of real uncertainty in the UK. John Major was two months away from his second turgid spell as Margaret Thatcher's political chauffeur. The month before the birth of the Premier League, the UK economy had continued to shed jobs at an alarming rate as it slogged through a recession and AIDS cases among heterosexuals had increased by 50 per cent in the previous year. Unemployment was flirting with the ten per cent barrier as songs like UB40's 'One in Ten' released the summer before reverberated and touched the nerve of many.

For so long stuck in a cultural rut, football now decided to go all in at being an aspect of popular culture. That first Premier League day, Shakespears Sister were number one with 'Stay', camp and gaudy lycra space odyssey *Star Trek VI: The Undiscovered Country* was about to be the UK's top box office film, Bush and Yeltsin had proclaimed an end to the Cold War two weeks before and the next day the US would lift its trade sanctions against China. No wonder the Premier League felt like a breath of helium and the start of something fresh. It was time to turn the colour dial up to 11. Who would have thought just a season or two earlier when kits were standard shades and designs we would be faced with a choice between 'ecru' (pale beige), powder blue, silver-grey, purple, lilac, jade, bottle green or denim? Gulp. But let's not forget that, in the 1872 FA Cup Final, Wanderers took to the field wearing pink, black and brown.

For the home kits that first Premier League season of 1992/93, Coventry seemed inspired by a winceyette nightie and Norwich City's Canaries looked to have eaten a bowl of custard and pack of seeds before throwing up all over the shirt. Some efforts were far more stylish and constrained. Blackburn and Arsenal had clean lines and Liverpool's bold three stripes were elegant decisions and subtle logo extensions for their kit manufacturers Adidas. However, this decision to effectively put the brand elements on each player's right shoulder was controversial with fans who felt the manufacturers were overwhelming the shirts, so this brand promotion by stealth was quietly dropped after 1995.

It was with the away kits for football's Brave New World that the hand brakes really came off. Arsenal's 'bruised banana' vibe had already

started. The garish confidence that new money underwrote was echoed in the designers' psychobabble when justifying this assault on the eyes. Part acid house 1980s hangover, part box of chevrons thrown to the four winds, for the first time Arsenal (and so many other newly minted, TV money fuelled clubs) realised that fans really would buy just about anything that has their crest on. As Joshua Robinson recalls in *The Club*, Manchester United, '[Were] being constantly pestered by charlatans with moronic merchandise ideas – one of them pitched the club women's knickers emblazoned with the words, I SCORED IN THE STRETFORD END (United declined that particular opportunity).'

Villa realised that two kits simply weren't enough for a team fighting to secure European domination. Unfortunately, the club finishing a distant second to Manchester United that season seemed to spend too much time on the Brazilian-inspired gold third kit instead of their team. In the following season they would finish tenth, then 18th in 1994/95 to begin a bumpy two decades of trial by error. Only Sheffield Wednesday, QPR, Liverpool, Arsenal and Blackburn struggled manfully through the whole first Premier League season with just two kits, and this in a league that contained Oldham Athletic, whose third kit was truly gangrenous, Coventry and Wimbledon.

On 20 February 1992 the foundation of the Premier League created an atmosphere of heady optimism also felt by the players (and their agents) who, for those in the top tier at least, would see wages snowballing exponentially. It was football's financial Big Bang. The £304m Murdoch's BSkyB dropped on the project for a five-year deal is a tiny fraction of the latest one that, astonishingly, values each game at £9m but it was a seismic sum at the time that Sky was forced to pay after their poorly received UK launch in 1989 that lacked any rights to the national game.

The Premier League was trying just too hard to scream 'WE ARE DIFFERENT' when, watching the first few games, the kits and the coverage were the only things for fans to tell this wasn't the old First Division. So kits had to shout, 'We are a new product! Now put your hands in your pockets and start coughing up!'

Even the presenters were forced to sell the *Good Morning Britain* clothing colour range. As Jonathan Clegg relates in *The Club*:

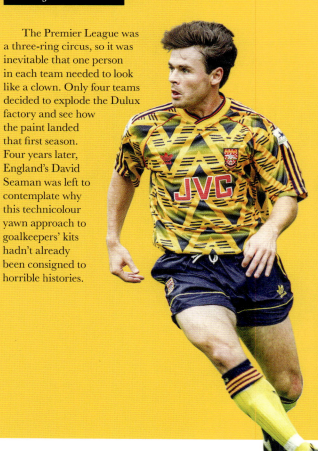

'They were deliberate. Do you think I really wanted to sit in green, pink, yellow, purple, blue, orange, white jackets? No!'

The Premier League was a three-ring circus, so it was inevitable that one person in each team needed to look like a clown. Only four teams decided to explode the Dulux factory and see how the paint landed that first season. Four years later, England's David Seaman was left to contemplate why this technicolour yawn approach to goalkeepers' kits hadn't already been consigned to horrible histories.

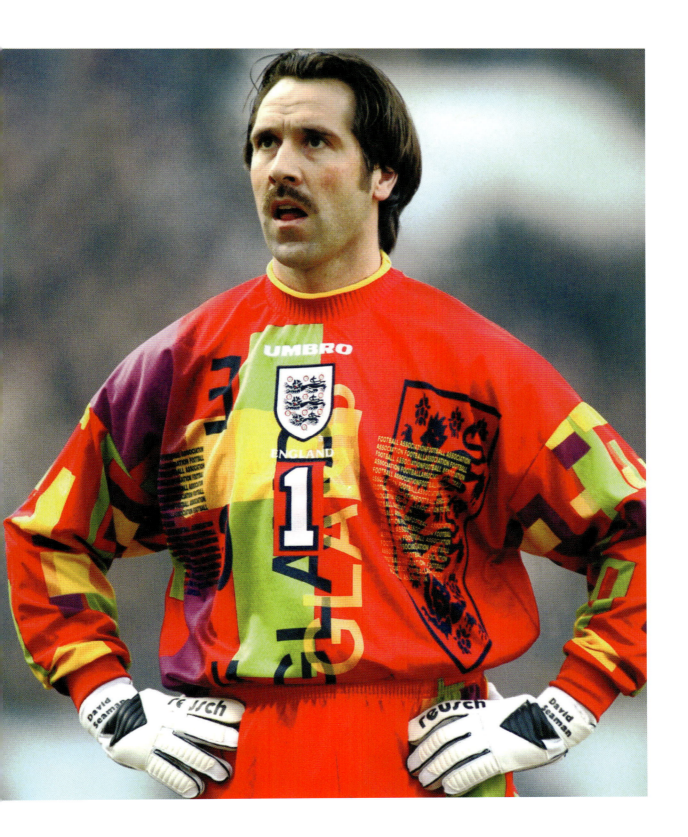

KIT&**CABOODLE**

Remarkably, for the Premier League curtain-raiser three of the teams – Norwich, Spurs and Manchester United – decided that their keepers needed a first and second kit, while Leeds slummed it with only one style. Oddly, the Leeds goalkeeper would clash with the blue away kit while Manchester United's Peter Schmeichel projected how the 1960s Jetsons thought clothes would look by 2000. Norwich's Bryan Gunn was lucky that, after the canary vomited home top, his two choices were conservative by comparison and Spurs' Ian Walker at least had the symmetry of each keeper's kit mirroring and alternating with the away and third kit.

Dan Baldassarre (@evornithology) has a superb Twitter thread that captures perhaps the true inspiration for these style dodgers. Birds. Seaman's soulmate was a Rainbow Lorikeet. The visual noise had been turned up to 11. David James was a Flame Bowerbird, and Dimitri Kharine was an American Goldfinch.

That first season saw plenty of global clubs wake up to the fact that, with a can-do 'all publicity is good publicity' attitude and new technology that allowed fever dreams full reign, anything – unfortunately – was possible. Schalke's home kit that year looked like something a scientist would tut at disapprovingly when squinting down his microscope. It wasn't only the fashion police that needed calling for Fiorentina's kit that season with its 'stylish' swastika ensemble on the sleeves.

Looking at the kits choices for 2021/22, there is so much more restraint. Like an ageing punk, the Premier League understands that they don't have enough hair to glue together a mohican and a nappy pin through the nose won't go down well at the next AGM. Tottenham's psychedelic away shirt is a horror show but the general colour palette is restrained and even, like Everton's away sash, elegant. There is only one other truly bonkers offering with Watford going full hornet for their home kit and one unforgivable choice with Manchester City's third kit ditching the club crest.

Some would say that Crystal Palace's Willy Wonka-inspired home kit also pushes the boundaries of sanity, especially for a 20st, pie-munching fan, but it has elements of joy and innovation. Other kit mistakes are fairly forgivable like Chelsea's Etch a Sketch on their home shirts and Liverpool's third kit McDonald's tribute. The sensible (not you, Spurs) kit choices reflect a game and society looking for new momentum. The world had been shut for over a year, the Premier League's telephone number figures were starting to be compared to doctors, nurses and caregivers while Peter Crouch's revelation in his excellent eponymous podcast that Premier League footballers are even provided with new game day underwear doesn't sit well with an increasing number of struggling supporters. Kits are more restrained in everything but price.

19

The Rise of the Retros

'Nostalgia ain't what it used to be.'

Yogi Berra

Retro shirt wearers are often, like me, hobbling into middle age. Writing for *When Saturday Comes* in February 2022, John Earls offered a staunch defence of the paunch often stretching the fabric of middle-aged replica kit wearers to breaking point.

For him, it demonstrates admirable commitment for a group who are disproportionately abused online for daring to say yes to dress that unforgivingly advertises the acres of extra timber now making up our middriff while opening us up to accusations of regressive infantile behaviour (as if that was a bad thing). As Earls explains:

'A more plausible reason for decrying kit wearers is that it's "childish". That's a claim with some historical basis. When replica kits were first on sale in the late 1970s, they were only in children's sizes; the first adult-sized England shirt didn't get manufactured until the 1982 World Cup's gorgeous chunky three-striped top. But forking out £50 a season doesn't just help your club's revenue, it helps keep in touch with the dreamer who just wants to forget their troubles for the next 90 minutes and be a fan.'

When the achingly quirky Half Man Half Biscuit sing 'All I Want For Christmas is a Dukla Prague Away Kit' they tap into how retro kits are a Rorschach inkblot test of our personalities. Created in the 1960s, this quirky process seems to come from the same synapses of Hermann Rorschach's brain as Adidas designers for Arsenal's bruised banana kit. A Rorschach test tells us nothing. The results are based on the reaction it receives. So, if the blot resembles a small cuddly bunny and your reaction is to visualise running amok with a ceremonial samurai sword in a busy town centre, then a clever psychologist, complex algorithms and their extensive knowledge base will suggest that the kindergarten teacher job may not be the one for you.

Buying timeless retro shirts are our way of rebelling against what John Nicholson calls the 'commodification of footballers brought about by the Premier League's money madness'. Retro shirts are also a chance to stick two fingers up to this week's iteration of the third change training kit or risk being less of a fan mentality. Even before buying one of the home or away 'official match' shirts at £100 a pop for the 2021/22 season, Arsenal fans have the privilege to buy a zip training top and 'Hype' training pants for £115, a pre-match shirt for £75, presentation jacket (whatever that is) for £65, training shirt, training tee and training top

for £130 and an anthem jacket (me neither) for £70. Oh, and to be clear, this isn't the first training range of the season. In Michael Calvin's inspiring and heartbreaking book *Whose Game is it Anyway?* he lays his size tens right into this merchandising moral blackmail:

'Notions of loyalty and family have been usurped and cheapened, most visibly, in Arsenal's case, in the promotion of the ultimate frivolity, a new third kit. The so-called authentic edition of the shirt sells for £100 as "a technical version" of the one "worn by your heroes on the pitch". Fans are urged to wear it "with pride and show your support for the Gunners".'

The clubs argue they are simply supplying a demand, but retro shirts serve to subvert the kneejerk impulse all us fans have to buy now and think later. It creates a feeling of calmness; a fixed and largely unsponsored point in time during this calamitous Covid epoch and 24/7 invasive online consumerism. Villa's elegant 1982 white pinstriped European Cup-winning shirt (stylishly celebrated in their 2021 away kit 40 years on) won't now require an electric custard presentation jacket to complete the authentic look. It is, and will always be, a receptacle of rose-tinted memories where we remember the victory but gloss over how we were dominated for huge swathes of the match by the Bayern Munich Machine or that, five short years later, we would be relegated. A feat immortalised in the Villa banner, 'From Rotterdam to Rotherham.'

Retro kits also give us free rein to wear football's most stylish creations. A modern-day Liverpool fan is unlikely to wear a present-day Italy shirt, but the achingly stylish AC Milan of the 2006 season or the 1974/5 Netherlands shirt (graced by those timeless magicians Cruyff and Neeskens) are a free pass to respect another team from afar. This also helps us scratch our collector's itch to overfill drawers and cupboards with Cameroon 1990, Milan 2002, France 1998 or Brazil 1970 among many, many more. Retro shirts also either let you escape the age of shirt sponsorship entirely or avoid ubiquitous betting logos for more stylish choices. Unfortunately for Joe Jordan at AC Milan, in 1981, their sponsor, Pooh Jeans, felt like a critique of his six goals in his first season that guided them to relegation to Serie B. To be fair to him (something you would always wisely be as even at the ripe old age of 50 he went headbutt to headbutt with the rottweiler captain of his former team, Gennaro Gattuso) he guided them back to the summit the following year as champions and top-scored.

Retro shirts resonate a purity, not only of design but intention. There was a kind of half-hearted appeal to take notice

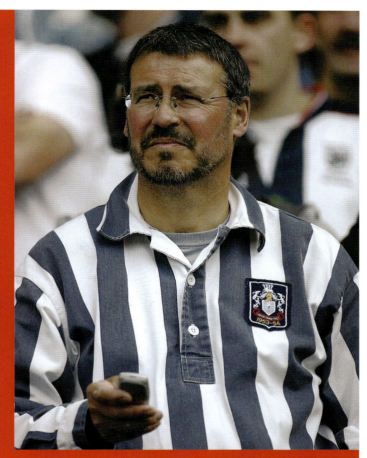

of any sponsorship diffidently offered rather than grabbing us by the throat Gattuso style. It was often more of an unwise financial decision by companies lending clubs a helping hand. Stadiums, the FA Cup, shirt sleeves and guerrilla marketing were all off limits. The return on investment for these companies was more often about connecting with the club and networking on boozy, smoke-filled Saturday evenings than driving up share prices, pernicious betting 'partnership opportunities' and aggressively expanding market share through debt-fuelled leveraged buyouts. That sense of community may have largely migrated online; it still exists in a supportive way, despite all the trolls and haters that infect most of our anti-social media screens.

Tweets 112K   Following 54.3K   Followers 6.29M

Manchester City ✔
@ManCity

The official Manchester City Twitter

Tweets   Tweets & replies

Pinned Tweet

Manchester City ✔ @ManCi
Sixteen players across eight n

Tweets 46.4K   Following 105   Followers 18.3M

Manchester United ✔
@ManUtd

Official account. More news and features

Tweets   Tweets & replies

Pinned Tweet

Manchester United ✔ @ManUt
Here they are – #MUFC's 2018/1

Tweets 1,048   Following 153   Followers 6.29M   Likes 10

amed Salah ✔
lah

r for Liverpool FC and Egypt

Tweets   Tweets & replies   Media

Mohamed Salah ✔ @MoSalah · Jun 12
I wear these for 100 million Egyptians. @adid

Revenge of the nerds

Did you know that in League Two up to 22 March 2022 there had been 79 different kits worn with one addition, a Colchester United tribute to Ukraine that would mark their fourth kit of the season? Or did you know that Forest Green had changed kits five times in eight games? Perhaps you had a hunch that, according to OptaJoe, 43 per cent of players wearing gloves win 50-50 duels or that, by 3 April, Newcastle United had played in seven kit variations in the same season. Part of me really hopes you don't.

Welcome to the comforting rabbit hole of football geekery. No minuscule tidbit is too forensic for this band of footballing uber-nerds. Twitter feeds like @kit_geek, @footballshirt or even @museumofjerseys swap stories in ever-decreasing circles. There is something compellingly innocent and heartfelt about this community of trend spotters swapping stories that fly well below the radar of vacuous mainstream media, preening players and their vampiric agents. There is clearly an audience for this heartfelt football kit fandom too. The Museum of Jerseys has over 25,000 followers, Football Geek has over 10,000 and Football Shirt Culture over 16,000. The numbers may seem minuscule compared to the ghost Twitter account of Cristiano Ronaldo's 94 million but rather than gawking at a one-man CR7 corporation, football kit geeks are highly active in a self-sustaining culture of community over commerce.

At the Non-League Football Shop there is even a subscription service where, for £30 a month, you can get a dozen non-league shirts a year giving you the chance to receive anything from a Boreham Wood purple goalkeeper shirt to a Grimsby Town shirt. There is even a mystery box of five non-league programmes for a fiver which is an achingly attractive offer that pitches us into a gloriously prelapsarian pre-Premier League universe. When you see the price of a Premier League shirt pegged at £70 before the confetti of upselling letters and patches, there is a magnetic nostalgia about diving into a land that Sky forgot.

The podcast world also serves as a balm for data itches. The surreal experience of an accountant passionately going through amortisation, post balance sheet events and contingent liabilities to a faithful following and over three million downloads are mesmerising. But what makes it mind-blowing is that I, like so many others, can't wait for the next biweekly podcast from Liverpool University lecturer Kieran Maguire while fellow host Kevin Day fights through another three-day hangover on *The Price of Football*. These people are becoming superstars of spreadsheets, the captains of consolidated accounts. Maguire has been called at home by former Prime Minister Gordon Brown to pick his brains about betting levies and there is the key. These people are not only passionate followers – Day of Crystal Palace and Maguire of Brighton – who broadcast fandom informed by intelligence. They are not spin doctors or product placers (their Manscape sponsorship was short-lived probably because of their irreverent puns about where the manscaping is done). Their ideas have heft and resonance, passion underscored by pragmatism.

Is this some form of magical lockdown madness where time-rich stay-at-homers seek out facts over spin and intelligence over secondary commentators' cretinous descriptions of what we can already see through the miracle of eyesight? Or is it a glorious sharing of the football passion that would shiver the oily black heart of Florentino Pérez and his cohort of billionaire goons? Whatever is feeding this compellingly uncool collective, let's embrace and celebrate them as we stumble, bleary-eyed and tracksuit trousered out of lockdown. The Greedy Six's patronising platitudes about the 'football pyramid' have one thing right. The strength is at the bottom and it's mighty lonely at the top.

Classic kits pique a nostalgic response for fans about a long-gone season or a golden era for their club and often reflect on their lives when they might have first worn the shirt. It creates wonderful flexibility where we can coordinate a positive period of our lives to a successful time for our club. The stars don't have to align: we can create the connection ourselves. So, I could buy my Villa 1981 First Division title-winning shirt in 1994 when I first met my wife and not have to buy that year's kit that celebrated 18th place and a brush with relegation.

Michael Maxwell tapped into this wonky alignment of personal and club success when he founded The Football Shirt Collective with a few friends in 2014. Since then, it has grown to become a community where people nostalgically obsess about old kits.

'We realised it was a really emotive thing,' he says. 'We wanted a place for the shirts and the stories behind the shirts.'

Scrolling through their website in April 2022 I am invited to buy a Venezia sponsor-free shirt, a NASA-inspired Orange Sun Jersey concept kit or a Your First Football Shirt A3 poster. Their 20,000 Twitter followers also actively scour the world for strange, stylish, or leaked new kit designs to pore over and share. Any supporter can find some joy to merge their personal and fandom lives if they look hard enough.

20

Who Are You?

When I give lectures in marketing at Exeter University, two things often happen:

- The students catch up on social media time
- The seats nearest the plug sockets become the most valuable so they can watch that film without battery anxiety

Meanwhile, at the front of the hall, I am gamely wading through theories and case studies they will need to neatly regurgitate in different forms a few months down the line. One of the key processes a few of my students will be giving their divided attention to is that of the Family Lifecycle Concept. Put briefly, it is an idealised overview of our target audience that puts them in neat boxes based on their stage of life. We would tend to segment these descriptions further into a more detailed customer profile to create a highly focussed breakdown into the person, how they behave and how they might respond to our product or service. Are you still listening at the back? In essence, how do we hatch, match and dispatch the consumption impulse?

Unlike buying a block of cheese, your football shirt purchase motivation is much more emotionally charged. Our price sensitivity for an Ollie Watkins shirt drops enormously after his perfect hat-trick against Liverpool but increases in his barren spells. But then there is another layer. Having watched him play for Exeter as a raw 19-year-old I am all in on the Ollie train. I might scour Money Saving Expert Martin Lewis's website for ways to save on my bills, but for Devon's finest he had me at 'latest edition'.

So, a Lifecycle Concept looks to put our whole purchasing existence into a team of 11 neat boxes from the quaintly titled Batchelor at one end of the scale to the rather sinister-sounding Solitary Survivor, Retired at the other. Let's have a look at some of these categories and the type of kit decisions they are likely to make at each age. So, a Batchelor is described as having flown the nest with few financial burdens who looks to fashion opinion leaders and is 'recreation orientated'. Two steps later and she is suddenly in the Full Nest 1 stage focussing strongly on buying a house, has a child under six and low levels of savings. Luckily for her, things start to look up in Full Nest 3 as part of an older married couple with dependent children creating a stronger financial situation. Unfortunately, according to marketing stereotyping, that is as good as it gets because, in another couple of stumbling steps, there is a drastic cut in income due to retirement and she will spend what little money she can find on medical products for her ever-increasing range of infirmities. So, as we meet our terminal lifecycle stage, we are now alone and spending what we can on cruise holidays, nursing home services and, gulp, funeral plans.

A Batchelor is a high target for football clubs as they are more likely to be swayed by new trends and have the disposable income or access to credit that allows them to make poorly thought through phone scrolling decisions. Who could bat for this team more effectively than one of the Arsenal Fan TV crew? I'm fascinated by Ty from the highly divisive and oddly masochistic show. Not only because he wears two pairs of Arsenal logoed earphones (one for the official Arsenal commentary and one for the BBC version) but that his every dressing decision is made inside the Arsenal merchandising universe. He entered a bubble long before Covid and his was based in the Arsenal superstore.

The way he dresses and acts display all the classic signs of neuroticism. I can only assume that he has a complex matchday dressing ritual spanning several hours where every element of his dress choices has to be addressed with a ceremonial gravitas that will materially affect the Gooners' performance later that day.

I'm a Full Nest 3 box filler described, faintly patronisingly as 'an older married couple' (I was born in the same year as Daniel Craig!) with two children who have part-time work. My spending focus is supposed to be trained on 'non-essential home appliances'. I would say I am a peak retro shirt target. The expanding midlife girth and helpful age-related fashion advice from my better 80 per cent will always nudge me towards the comfortingly copious cotton of Villa's 1982 European Cup-winning shirt and the even more forgivingly tailored 1956 beauty when players in the team probably shared my vital statistics. If my wife's suggestions don't move me on from polyester folly, Michael Calvin's passionately held view certainly does, 'Those ludicrously expensive shirts are not aimed at my generation, despite plenty of my contemporaries entering their third childhood, deluding themselves that they look stylish as they squeeze into them. They put unfair pressure on parents, whose children are sucked into a culture of false expectation.'[10]

Ouch.

[10]Calvin, M., *Whose Game Is It Anyway?: Football, Life, Love & Loss*, p258-259 (Pitch Publishing, Kindle edition)

There is a football team of boxes to put us in from the shave to the grave, so let's have a look at our team of Top Trumps and how they measure up.

MARRIED, NO KIDS

Accommodation Independence:	80
Earning Power:	86
Spending Power:	90
Online Activity:	78
Peer Pressure:	70
Shirt Sales Rating:	84

YOUNG SINGLES

Accommodation Independence:	15
Earning Power:	35
Spending Power:	72
Online Activity:	93
Peer Pressure:	90
Shirt Sales Rating:	94

NEWLY MARRIED COUPLES

Accommodation Independence:	40
Earning Power:	55
Spending Power:	76
Online Activity:	80
Peer Pressure:	75
Shirt Sales Rating:	65

FULL NEST 2
THE KIDS HAVE STARTED SCHOOL

Accommodation Independence:	65
Earning Power:	50
Spending Power:	40
Online Activity:	55
Peer Pressure:	35
Shirt Sales Rating:	30

FULL NEST 1 (NEW PARENTS)

Accommodation Independence:	60
Earning Power:	60
Spending Power:	24
Online Activity:	30
Peer Pressure:	40
Shirt Sales Rating:	28

FULL NEST 3
THE KIDS MIGHT BE WORKING FULL TIME

Accommodation Independence:	60
Earning Power:	55
Spending Power:	30
Online Activity:	50
Peer Pressure:	30
Shirt Sales Rating:	25

OLDER SINGLES

Accommodation Independence:	75
Earning Power:	60
Spending Power:	26
Online Activity:	80
Peer Pressure:	76
Shirt Sales Rating:	70

EMPTY NEST 1

Accommodation Independence:	90
Earning Power:	87
Spending Power:	90
Online Activity:	78
Peer Pressure:	40
Shirt Sales Rating:	72

EMPTY NEST 2

Accommodation Independence:	80
Earning Power:	89
Spending Power:	45
Online Activity:	60
Peer Pressure:	20
Shirt Sales Rating:	16

SOLITARY SURVIVOR

Accommodation Independence:	20
Earning Power:	14
Spending Power:	10
Online Activity:	70
Peer Pressure:	10
Shirt Sales Rating:	9

RETIRED SOLITARY SURVIVOR
Club Atletico de Madrid - Muangthong United TOO 28/10/2010

Accommodation Independence:	15
Earning Power:	10
Spending Power:	7
Online Activity:	75
Peer Pressure:	WHAT IS THAT?
Shirt Sales Rating:	5

Football fans of any age also need to be consumers with the stretchiest Elasticity of Demand. The process describes how, for some goods (like that block of cheese) when it reaches a certain price, we will choose something else because our demand is elastic. Cheese is just cheese after all. But for football shirts, it's a completely different approach. Our demand becomes dementedly inelastic. We buy the same amount of the product irrespective of whether the price drops (last year's kit) or rises (everything else). This situation is supposed to describe our purchase of essential items like petrol and food but, as we know, in football logical budgeting are dirty words. If, after eating the cheese you got sick, you would never buy more of it to support the company because they must really be struggling, what with all those people they poisoned. But a fan of Manchester City in 2021 will buy the shirt to associate herself with the way the club is going gangbusters but also bought the shirt in the dark 1980s days of a club intent on perpetual self-harm as a perverse way (and I was on the Kippax then so I know how perverse City fans could be) of showing you are a loyal supporter. It's a blessing for the kit makers, if not for the cheesemakers.

The guru of group relief Kieran Maguire illustrates demand elasticity with his usual clarity and authority in his definitive book on football finance, *The Price of Football*:

'For example, a retailer called Jones sells, on average, 200 Liverpool shirts a week at £50 each. He then decides to increase the price to £60. None of the other retailers nearby increase their prices from the original £50. As a result, Jones' sales of Liverpool shirts fall to 80 per week.

His price elasticity of demand is calculated as:
Percentage change in demand for Liverpool shirts $= (80 - 200)/ 200 = -60\%$
Percentage change in price for Liverpool shirts $= (60 - 50)/ 50 = 20\%$
Price elasticity is therefore 3 (60%/20%) (economists ignore the negative sign). The reason why elasticity of demand is important to a seller is that if elasticity at the present price point is greater than 1, then an increase in price will lead to a decrease in total sales income.'[11]

Dismissing people who buy football shirts as indulging in vanity and financial insanity says more about the accusers than the accused. This sweeping rejection of our choices underestimates the power football shirts hold to reveal who we really are in ways mainstream fashion can only ape or ignore. As fashion designer Martine Rose shared with *The Face* in chapter three, those personal reflections and questions can

[11] Maguire Kieran, *The Price of Football: Understanding Football Club Finance*, p77 (Agenda Publishing, Kindle edition)

be uncomfortable, but by challenging ourselves we can effect real change just as Tromsø did. They knew that silence and compliance would have been the point of least resistance, but they chose a different path and the difficult issues it raised made them learn much more about themselves, their club, their community and their country than meek complicity to a profoundly flawed World Cup ever would.

Rose explained, 'I like decorative things, of course. But, for me anyway, as a designer I like to exist where you're not sure if you like it or not, or you're not sure if it's going to work, or you have to ask yourself a lot of questions about it. That sense of unease, that's where I know I like it.'

People like Mark Zuckerberg and Elizabeth Holmes may wear black to free up vital 'bandwidth' for their alpha brains (Holmes will be wearing prison orange for some time though) but their binary fashion decision is driven by their egos and a determination not to reveal who they are beneath their billions and what they believe.

The kaleidoscope of matchday shirts gives telling insights into our true personalities. On Exeter matchdays at St James Park there are retros, latest editions, shirts that were bought a few tummy sizes ago and homemade editions in club colours. Each one is a personality fingerprint of the fan and the values they hold dear. It makes some of us look odd (check out

Exeter's purple 1992/93 creation and try not to look away) but it tells our story in ways that High Street fashion never could. Mainstream shirts tap into the ephemeral trends of a single season before the next design comes along, but football fans choose how long their shirts tell their story. My Las Palmas 2017/18 polo shirt brings back memories of living on the island watching a rare top-flight season that ended in relegation but sun-filled memories. When it gets frayed I simply buy an identical copy to recharge the memories of warm evenings watching games with a tropical beer in a stunning stadium (and mediocre football).

There is something magnetically rebellious about us choosing what we consume rather than walking the treadmill of seasonal fashion advice. We can dip in and out of the club's offerings to suit our personalities and get inspiration from a much broader canvas than those trying to be persistently 'on point'. If it makes us look out of kilter with the current trends then, for this middle-aged man, that is more than good enough for me.

Acknowledgements

Kevin Day has been a real legend, despite his incredibly busy schedule as a comedian, scriptwriter for *Have I Got News for You* and presenter of podcast *The Price of Football*. I'm also really grateful to Scott Palfrey and Craig Bratt, the media team at Exeter City, Kit and Bone's Matt Pascoe, Daley Jones for sharing the story of his annual disgusting kit competition and John Devlin for sharing his research on the history of Melchester Rovers' kits.

To Jonny from Icarus, I really appreciate your time and input to the book and the shirts you kindly made for me. Thanks to Phil Delves for sharing his thought-provoking blog about the dangers of shirt collecting addiction. Thanks to Tania Harding and Jayme Sporton from Football Shirts For Charity for allowing me to share their story. Mike from The Football Shirt Collective was also incredibly helpful, as was Gavin Hope from @museumofjerseys for his updates.

Now a Fair Game colleague, it was great to get the inside story of how Charlton have supported LGBT+ football from Zaki Dogliani, Charlton's Community Trust marketing and communications manager. Ric Dennis from merchandise company Hope and Glory and Scott Gordon from NI Mugs are so passionate about their work that it's infectious. Former Leyton Orient CEO Danny Macklin always has time to help, especially with stories about the club he so passionately led.

To the legends that are Caz and Lucy and the team of Her Game Too, I can only apologise for the Neanderthal minority of men plaguing our game, but thank you for all your help.

Football shirt culture is filled with so many passionate enthusiasts across the country and so many of them were generous with their time and content for this book. To @kitandbone I really appreciate your giving me advice and feedback about their designs. To Kieran and his crew at the fantastic @soccersartorial, they gave me real inspiration with their fantastic content. I also really appreciate the help and feedback from @JARK_Production and the passion and help given by @fsfcuk and Michael Maxwell, founder of The Football Shirt Collective.